God Formed Us
For His Glory

Joel S. Goldsmith

Edited by
Lorraine Sinkler

Acropolis Books, Publisher
Atlanta, Georgia

Published by Acropolis Books
All rights reserved
Printed in the United States of America

For information contact:
ACROPOLIS BOOKS, INC.
Atlanta, Georgia

www.acropolisbooks.com

Cover and text design: Tonya Beach Creative Services

Library of Congress Cataloging-in-Publication Data

Goldsmith, Joel S., 1892-1964.
  God formed us for his glory / Joel S. Goldsmith ; edited by Lorraine
Sinkler.
      p. cm.
  ISBN 1-889051-67-5
  1. Spiritual life. I. Sinkler, Lorraine. II. Title.

  BP610.G641558 2004
  299'.93--dc22

                              2003025987

Except the Lord build the house,
they labour in vain that build it. . .

– Psalm 127

Illumination dissolves all material ties and binds men together with the golden chains of spiritual understanding; it acknowledges only the leadership of the Christ; it has no ritual or rule but the divine, impersonal universal Love; no other worship than the inner Flame that is ever lit at the shrine of Spirit. This union is the free state of spiritual brotherhood. The only restraint is the discipline of Soul; therefore, we know liberty without license; we are a united universe without physical limits, a divine service to God without ceremony or creed. The illumined walk without fear – by Grace.

–*The Infinite Way* by Joel S. Goldsmith

Dedication

Twentieth century mystic Joel S. Goldsmith revealed to the Western world the nature and substance of mystical living that demonstrated how mankind can live in the consciousness of God. The clarity and insight of his teachings, called the Infinite Way, were captured in more than thirty-five books and in over twelve hundred hours of tape recordings that, today, perpetuate his message.

Joel faithfully arranged to have prepared from his class tapes, monthly letters which were made available as one of the most important tools to assist students in their study and application of the Infinite Way teachings. He felt each of these letters came from an ever-new insight that would produce a deeper level of understanding and awareness of truth as students worked diligently with this fresh and timely material.

Each yearly compilation of the *Letters* focused on a central theme, and it became apparent that working with an entire year's material built an ascending level of consciousness. The *Letters* were subsequently published as books, each containing all the year's letters. The publications became immensely popular as they proved to be of great assistance in the individual student's development of spiritual awareness.

Starting in 1954, the monthly letters were made availiable to students wishing to subscribe to them. Each year of the *Letters* was published individually during 1954 through 1959 and made available in book form. From 1960 through 1970 the *Letters* were published and renamed as books with the titles:

1960 Letters	*Our Spiritual Resources*
1961 Letters	*The Contemplative Life*
1962 Letters	*Man Was Not Born to Cry*
1963 Letters	*Living Now*
1964 Letters	*Realization of Oneness*
1965 Letters	*Beyond Words and Thoughts*
1966 Letters	*The Mystical I*
1967 Letters	*Living Between Two Worlds*
1968 Letters	*The Altitude of Prayer*
1969 Letters	*Consciousness Is What I Am*
1970 Letters	*Awakening Mystical Consciousness*

Joel worked closely with his editor, Lorraine Sinkler, to ensure each letter carried the continuity, integrity, and pure consciousness of the message. After Joel's transition in 1964, Emma A. Goldsmith (Joel's wife) requested that Lorraine continue working with the monthly letters, drawing as in the past from the inexhaustible tape recordings of his class work with students. The invaluable work by Lorraine and Emma has ensured that this message will be preserved and available in written form for future generations. Acropolis Books is honored and privileged to offer in book form the next eleven years of Joel's teaching.

The 1971 through 1981 *Letters* also carry a central theme for each year, and have been renamed with the following titles:

1971 Letters	*Living by the Word*
1972 Letters	*Living the Illumined Life*
1973 Letters	*Seek Ye First*
1974 Letters	*Spiritual Discernment: the Healing Consciousness*
1975 Letters	*A Message for the Ages*
1976 Letters	*I Stand on Holy Ground*
1977 Letters	*The Art of Spiritual Living*
1978 Letters	*God Formed Us for His Glory*
1979 Letters	*The Journey Back to the Father's House*
1980 Letters	*Showing Forth the Presence of God*
1981 Letters	*The Only Freedom*

Acropolis Books dedicates this series of eleven books to Lorraine Sinkler and Emma A. Goldsmith for their ongoing commitment to ensure that these teachings will never be lost to the world.

Table of Contents

God Formed Us
For His Glory

Chapter One

Introduction to the
Spiritual Plane

The three dimensional world includes the physical and the mental planes of life, but the spiritual plane is the fourth dimensional. If we live on the physical level of life there are specific laws: laws of food, laws of diet, laws of exercise, laws of medicine, which must be observed or we may get into trouble. For example, if a person living on the physical plane of life were to remain sitting in a chair all the time, he would soon find himself losing the use of many of the functions of his body. On that level of life, it is important to follow some of the laws requiring intelligent diet, adequate exercise, and sufficient fresh air.

Then there is the mental plane. The Master, Christ Jesus, admonished those on that plane that not only is the act of adultery a sin, but the very thought of it is, indicating that a mental activity is as much an error of life as the physical act itself. On the mental plane, too, there are mental causes for physical conditions, and mental science is largely based on that premise. If a person worries he gets ulcers, and if he is jealous, envious, or hateful, he may get a cancer, and if he is resentful, he may get rheumatism. An entire metaphysical practice grew up dedicated to the idea that if the mental fault could be discovered, physical ills could be cured.

Later on, some forms of *materia medica* adopted the same premise that some mental activity within a person is responsible for a particular physical disorder in his experience. This idea has become the basis of much psychological and psychiatric practice, and has been so widely accepted that many metaphysical practitioners first try to find the error in a person's thought and thereby remove the effects from his body.

If we are living out from the physical plane, it is wise to follow the laws of matter. If we have in some measure transcended the physical plane to where we have been able to accept life on a more mental level, it is wise to watch our thoughts and, if we are indulging in envy, hate, jealousy, malice, greed, or lust, to try to overcome such thoughts and hold ourselves on a higher plane of consciousness.

I do not contend that living on either the physical or the mental plane is wrong, but I ask you not to think that the spiritual plane is wrong, either, or that it is impractical, until you have experienced it. The message of the Infinite Way is primarily spiritual. It ignores many of the things and thoughts that are important on the physical and mental level.

Take No Thought for the Things of This World

On the physical plane of life a person usually works hard physically, very often by the sweat of his brow, to earn his daily bread. On the mental plane a person uses far less of muscle and bodily strength but engages more in mental activities, not only the mental activities that concern his particular position, activity, or profession in life, but even mental forms of prayer to enhance the prosperity of the activity.

On the spiritual plane, that changes. On the spiritual plane of life, it is not necessary to earn a living; it is not necessary to work for a living; it is not even necessary to do anything about making a living. That sounds ideal, doesn't it, and quite an advance? But let us not be fooled by it. When we come to the spiritual way of life we work harder than we ever did on the physical or the mental, only now instead of working for a living, we are working because something has been given us to do of a nature that we must do, and our living comes in as incidental to the work. We are now beginning to approach that place in life spoken of by the Master, when he said, "Take no thought for your life, what ye shall eat; neither for the body, what ye shall put on."[1] He tells us very clearly that the nations of the world, that is, the people of the mental and physical realm, take thought for these things but not those aspiring to live the spiritual life.

We must not take thought for what we shall eat or what we shall drink or wherewithal we shall be clothed. We must take thought only for the things of God. We must take thought only for the revelation or realization of God, and what we eat, drink, and are clothed with will be added unto us. Now we enter quite a different degree of consciousness because we are not seeking physically or mentally for anything of this life: not supply, not companionship, not home, not happiness, not peace, not joy, not security. Now we are seeking only the realization of God and then finding that in the attaining of it all of these things are added unto us.

The Conflict Between the Humanly Good and the Humanly Bad

In this twentieth century the world is still busy seeking safety, security, and peace as if the experience of the centuries preceding the era of the Master were not enough to convince it that finding safety, security, and peace is impossible. Those thing never have been found since the world began, and furthermore, those things are never going to be found, because there is no such thing in this world as safety, security, or peace.

On the physical or mental plane of life, men and women will

always be caught in the two opposing or conflicting powers called good and evil. There will be good human beings and there will be bad human beings. As long as that is true, the bad ones will try to benefit at the expense of the good ones, and the good ones will have to fight back to protect themselves from the bad ones. So in a world where there are good men and women and bad men and women there will be strife and a lack of security.

The human race is partly good and partly evil. Those who are the good seek safety, security, and peace and are willing for all men and women to have it. There never has been a people on earth who wanted war. Always it was the minority or evil ones who brought the peace loving majority into these conflicts. There is no answer to this problem on the human plane, but there is an answer on the spiritual plane.

An Arm of Flesh

When the Hebrews were besieged by an enemy stronger than they, they rushed to their leader, "The enemy is stronger than we are. They have multitudes; they have hordes."

Hezekiah, their leader, replied, "Be strong and courageous, be not afraid nor dismayed for the king of Assyria, nor for all the multitude that is with him: for there be more with us than with him: With him is an arm of flesh; but with us is the Lord our God to help us."[2] He might have continued and said that in the presence of the Lord God Almighty "an arm of flesh" is not a power. A short time after that, the enemy used their arms to fight, wipe out, and destroy each other.

David found himself in a similar position when Goliath faced him encased in heavy armor, and in addition to his heavy defense of armor, he had an offensive weapon. They tried to put a coat of mail on David, but his answer was, "I cannot go with these; for I have not proved them. . . . This day will the Lord deliver thee into mine hand. . . for the battle is the Lord's."[3] Then he went out against this mighty armor with nothing but an insignificant little pebble. Nevertheless he was master of the situation.

To human sense blindness is an indisputable power, but the Master with this spiritual wisdom and vision thought so little of the power of blindness that he took spittle, an emblem of disdain, a nothingness, and healed a blind man with spittle, with that which is no power, that which no Hebrew would honor as worthy of anything. With this nothingness the Master healed what appeared as the power of blindness.

Turn to God for God-Awareness

On the spiritual plane of life, anything and everything to which you have given power on the material or mental plane, you now turn upon with as much indifference as you would to a pebble or spittle: "You are no power, because in the presence of God there is but one power"—not one power that overcomes error, but one power in the presence of which there is no form of error, no weapon that can be formed against you that can prosper. The whole secret lies in seeking the kingdom of God, in the presence of which nothing else is power.

In the message of the Infinite Way, there is never a turning to God for the overcoming of sin, disease, or lack. There is a turning to God continually for the purpose of living, moving, and having our being in God. In the consciousness of God's presence, regardless of the strength of the enemy, that strength is but "an arm of flesh,"a nothingness, no power. It is a no law, a no cause. This is one of the major principles that brought about the writing of the book, *The Infinite Way*.[4] I had witnessed many attempts to overcome error, to use right thinking to overcome wrong thinking; but I found, even in my own experience, that nothing I could do in the way of right thinking would overcome my wrong thinking because something within me was predisposed toward wrong thinking, and no power would change that.

The realization finally came that I needed no power to

remove the error, sins, discords, and inharmonies. I needed but one thing: to come into the presence of the living God, to attain an awareness of God, an actual conscious communion with God. Then I would be in the presence of that which is itself infinite, eternal, immortal, and besides which there is nothing else. And so it proved to be.

The Branch and the Vine

There are dozens of passages in scripture that reveal that a realization of God leaves one in a world without sin, disease, lack, or limitation. Most of the people on earth are not sinners. They are moderately good, moral persons, in no way bad enough to deserve the horrors that have been visited upon them in every generation. No one has the right to say that you and I are so evil that we deserve plagues of polio, hydrogen bombs thrown at us, or incarceration in concentration camps. None of us is that evil, not even humanly. Why is it then that the world fights the problem of human discord from the cradle to the grave? Why is it that innocent young mothers suffer and sometimes die in the very act of giving birth? Why all this? And the world has no answer for it except to say that it does not know.

But in the 15th Chapter of John, the Master gave us an answer as to why the world is experiencing discord. He points out that we are the branches, Christ is the vine, and God is the Father, the source, the essence. The vine is one with its source and if the branches abide in the vine, then harmony flows.

Picture a tree with the branches on the tree all connected with the central trunk and let us call that the vine, and then realize down below in the ground is the root which is in contact with the whole earth. As long as the branch is on the tree, it is at-one with the vine and the trunk, and as long as that trunk is established in the earth, that tree will bear fruit richly because through the roots and the trunk the elements and substances necessary to the formation of the fruits will be distributed and in due time the fruitage will appear.

But what happens if the branch is cut off from the trunk and laid on the ground? For a short while it keeps on living on the substance that is already within, but it is not being renewed day by day. Instead, it is using itself up. So in time it withers and bears no more fruit. So with us.

As human beings we may live out our human span of three-score years and ten, ten less or ten more. We have used up the little life with which we started and the little more we added through our food and drink, but the end was a withering up and a dying and a looking back on our lives, wondering, "Why was I born? Why did I come to earth? What have I ever done to repay my mother's birth pangs?" In most cases the answer is that we have not contributed much to the world, not done much to justify our existence on earth.

Being Spiritually Sustained

No saint, seer, prophet, or savior who came to the realization that by living in God he was eternally fed by a hidden spring, a hidden well of water, spiritual bread and meat ever testified to the futility of life. Christ Jesus described that inner sustenance in this way: "I have meat to eat that ye know not of.[5] . . . Whosoever drinketh of the water that I shall give him shall never thirst; but the water that I shall give him shall be in him a well of water springing up into everlasting life.[6] . . . I am the bread of life."[7] In other words, the Master revealed a substance which he called meat, water, and bread, but which was not material. When he said, "I am the bread of life," he was not talking about a baker's loaf of bread because obviously he was not that. When he spoke of bread, meat, wine, and water, this inner water that springs up into life eternal, he was speaking of a spiritual source of supply, a spiritual source of life, a spiritual source of substance and activity, having which we have everything on the outer plane.

The principle of the Infinite Way is that we have within our being that which Jesus called the bread, the wine, and the water but which we will call the Christ.

I acknowledge God to be the
very temple of my being.

I acknowledge God to be the light,
the soul, the spirit,
the animating principle of my being.

I acknowledge that the
entire kingdom of God
is active in my consciousness and
that it is appearing outwardly
as the happiness, joy, success,
supply, home, the allness
of my daily experience.

The moment that we do that we no longer have to take anxious thought for our living, nor do we have to worry about a home, companionship, safety, security, or peace, because, having found this center of being to be God, we carry with us our peace.

There is no peace external to me.
The peace is within me, and I express it.
If I express it to any person, the reflex action
of peace is coming back to me.
If I express love, justice, kindness, mercy,
it is inevitable that these
reflect themselves back to me.

But we first must let it flow out from us. We first must acknowledge that all of this is within us now, not by virtue of our great understanding or spirituality, but by virtue of the truth that as the branch we are one with the vine and the vine is one with God, all one: God the Father, God the son, God the Holy Ghost. In that oneness the spirit of God flows forth and appears on earth as the harmony of our being.

Security in God-Consciousness

Peace can come only in your consciousness and in mine. It cannot come from outside somewhere. There is nothing in any room that will bring peace or will give peace except what we are entertaining in consciousness. There is nothing in any room that could start a quarrel except what we may bring there in our consciousness. So there is no use ever to look outside ourselves for peace or security because we will not find them.

If we bring an awareness of God's presence to a place, the 91st Psalm will be demonstrated; "There shall no evil befall thee."[8] An objection might be raised, "Ah, but I have seen a lot of evil come nigh my dwelling place, or somebody else's dwelling place." That is because the very first verst of the 91st Psalm has been forgotten. "He that dwelleth in the secret place of the most High shall abide under the shadow of the Almighty."[9] The 91st Psalm does not promise that we will have protection as human beings: it promises us protection in the degree that we abide in the secret place of the most High. And so does the Master promise us that we will bear fruit richly only if we abide in the word and if we let the word abide in us.

Is it not clear now that the peace and harmony of our life are dependent upon an activity of our own consciousness? There is no God outside who can give us peace, safety, and security if we are violating Its laws, nor are there any legal laws, any national or international laws that can save us from any violation of spiritual law. The harmony of our individual life must somehow be found within us as an activity of our consciousness, as an unfoldment of truth within our consciousness, and we must expect it without any help from any person. Then when we have found it, we can share it with those who desire it and can open themselves to it. Eventually they, too, must open their own consciousness individually, specifically, and continuously to the operation of divine law within them.

How the World Will Be Saved

It is not that we have found a God that through our prayers or treatment will heal disease, sin, death, lack or limitation. Rather we have found that a realization of God's presence reveals no sin, no disease, no discord, no lack, or limitation in our experience. Only in this way can the world itself ultimately be saved from itself.

If I individually experience God as a reality and find that in entertaining God continuously in my consciousness the evils of life do not approach me, some member of my family, some friend, or some business acquaintance sees that, and it is not long before one or more of those becomes interested in a spiritual way of life. Then as I can demonstrate to them that a realization of God removes from them all of these human discords or, if not all, the vast majority of them and certainly the major ones, then they become a light and someone notices that in them and soon they, too, attract others to this way of life. This has been the experience of the Infinite Way. Beginning with one individual it soon was realized and experienced by friends, and so it has spread in these years to cover a goodly portion of the world.

If you are a businessman there should be good business, prosperous business, harmonious business. If you are an employer there should be harmonious relationships with employees. If you are an employee there should be harmonious relationships with employers. If you are a citizen of a free community you have to be able to live in harmony with your neighbors and with members of your nation. Thus it becomes important that we find some thing that will bring these experiences of harmony, not only into our human life so far as health is concerned, not only into our financial lives so far as economic abundance is concerned, but into every avenue of human relationships.

The Infinite Way has demonstrated that that is a present possibility. It has brought harmony between capital and labor; it has brought harmony into family relationships; it has brought harmony into communities; it has brought harmony into the lives of individuals, whether engaged in a business or a profession. God becoming an actual reality in our experience becomes that which reveals the absence of discords.

Do Not Battle Evil

In a realization of God, the discords and inharmonies of life begin to fade away. They may not all disappear in one day but they do disappear, and they not only disappear but they lead us into "green pastures"[10] and "beside the still waters."[10] They make an entirely new life for us. Paul summed it up in this way: "I live; yet not I, but Christ liveth in me."[11] That becomes an actual experience to us in which there is a presence within that gives us our daily work to do and establishes harmony in the working out of our work, whether it is housework, whether it is store work, professional work, or any other kind of work.

When God is accepted as one presence, one power without opposition, when God is accepted as the infinite and only, in that moment the so-called errors of sense begin to drop away. As long as we are battling the discords of earth we multiply them. There is a principle of scripture relative to not fighting evil,[12] not fighting it and not pulling up the weeds, but letting the tares and the wheat grow together, and then in their due time the tares fall away.[13] So it is with this. Without battling disease or laws of disease, without struggling for our livelihood, we can begin in any given moment of the day or night—it could be this minute—to relax in the realization:

God is one, and besides Him there is
no other, so I have nothing to fear as to
what mortal man can do to me.
I have nothing to fear as to what a mortal
condition can do to me.
No weapon that is formed against me can prosper.
In Him I live and move and have my being.
In Him is the eternality of life,
the immortality of being, protection,
harmony, completeness, wholeness.

To Know That God Is, Is Enough

Duality means twoness. The duality that perpetuates our discords is the belief in good and evil. If we believe in God and devil, if we believe in a power of God and a power of evil to which God can do something, or if we believe in the immortal and the mortal, we have the source of every discord that is in our experience. The moment that we accept the truth that God is one and God is all and God is infinite and, therefore, we do not have to fear what mortal man or mortal mind or mortal condition can do to us, if only we can accept that as an intellectual premise and hold to it consistently for a week, a month, six weeks, or nine weeks, the hard shell of the errors in our experience begin to crumble by a persistent holding to this truth in our consciousness:

God is one, and besides Him
there is no other. God is the only power.
Therefore I do not have
to fight the power of man,
the power of beast, the power of condition,
or the power of circumstances.
I accept God as infinite being.

Watch what a few weeks of a consistent holding to that truth will do to whatever hard crust of error is disturbing the harmony of your existence. Everyone must face the great doubt in his heart and soul: Is there really a God? Is there? I'd like to believe it, but I haven't seen too much evidence of It and sometimes I have trusted It and It didn't come through. Most persons of the world, while claiming a belief in God, actually do not believe. If they did they would show it forth in their life. If God is, isn't that enough? That should be the answer to all life. God is, and that is enough.

Do we really care for anything else on earth if we can receive an assurance within our own being that God is? Would we ever again fear? Would we ever again doubt? Would we ever again feel that it was of any concern to us whether temporarily we were making our bed in hell or whether temporarily we were walking in "the valley of the shadow of death?"[14]

No, "whither shall I go from thy spirit? or whither shall I flee from thy presence? . . .

If I make my bed in hell, behold, thou art there.

If I take the wings of the morning, and dwell in the uttermost parts of the sea;

Even there shall thy hand lead me, and thy right hand hold me."[15]

ACROSS THE DESK

All joy to you in this New Year as each day you let God dedicate the temple of your mind, body, and life to His glory.

Each monthly letter, as a statement of spiritual principles, is complete in itself, focusing on one spiritual principle and setting forth its application in daily experience. That is why it is important for students to study the letter throughout the month and consciously to put into practice its principle in their daily life. Thus students will be building a sure foundation on which the superstructure of spiritual awareness rests.

From now on "Across the Desk" will appear in the monthly letter only when there is some item of timely interest and significance. It will not be a regular feature.

All students can rejoice in the continued spread of the message throughout the world, with new persons daily discovering the writings and becoming a part of the Infinite Way consciousness of oneness which is making a "new heaven and new earth" a living reality.

TAPE RECORDED EXCERPTS
Prepared by the Editor

Life can only be lived today in this moment of nowness. Let that moment be lived in the awareness of God's all-sufficient grace which appears outwardly as the harmony of our experience. The following excerpts from the tape recordings, meditated upon and practiced until they come alive within us, can reveal to us the glories of each new day—not yesterday and not tomorrow, but today.

"Today"

"The New Year must be the product of what we make it. The New Year must be something that we start in operation this minute. It will not do to wait until midnight tonight; it will not do to start tomorrow. The type of year that we are to experience must be started now in this moment by an act of decision, and each one must make the decision for himself: Am I to be God-governed or man-governed this year? I must now choose whether I will serve God or man. If I am true to God, I need have no fear that I will be untrue to man, to my government, or to any government. . . that stands for the integrity of individual being, individual freedom, liberty, and justice. Therefore, I must take my stand for government under God. . . .

"I must at this moment acknowledge that only spiritual

power is power. I will be faced all year with the temptation of material powers, mental powers, and legal powers, but I must at this moment embrace in my acknowledgment the great truth that God is spirit, that the law of God is spiritual, and that *being* is spiritual and infinite; and being infinite, there is no power in any other law than the spiritual law which is embodied within me.

"I must acknowledge that the son of God, the *I* that I am, is my food, shelter, protection, fortress, hiding place, and abiding place. I do not seek in the external world, but rather do I realize that I embody all the good necessary to my experience throughout this year. At this moment I possess all that will be unfolding in my experience throughout the year. At this moment, it is embodied within me, embraced within my consciousness, and day by day, it will unfold. As it is necessary, it will appear in my human experience. There is nothing that I will need this coming year that is not already embraced in me.

"The reason that we are called upon to make this acknowledgment now, in this moment, is that every minute that passes is going to be a continuation of this minute, and what we put into this minute is what is going to be a continuing experience for us throughout eternity. All that is embraced in our consciousness now will continue to unfold unto eternity because there is no future time. Now, in the present, is the substance of that which unfolds to us as time, and it includes within it that which we are placing in it at this moment. . . .

"What you embody in your consciousness now unfolds as the next minute, the next hour, the next day, the next year. The truth that you embody in consciousness at this moment will be the continuing unfolding truth throughout all time. That which you do not embrace in your consciousness cannot appear tomorrow. . . .

"Infinite being is the nature of your being; infinite being is the capacity of your being, but now, in this moment, you must recognize this, acknowledge it, and submit yourself to it, and then each day remind yourself of it. Then this moment of your life becomes the continuing moment throughout this New Year which you are now, in this moment, making a happy, joyous, and prosperous one that no man can take from you. Even you will not be able to limit it to one year. It will be the Happy New Year of all the New Years to come on this side of the veil or another, for neither life nor death can separate you from the love of God, the life of God, and the consciousness of God, the awareness of which is now your being."

Joel S. Goldsmith, "New Year's Eve 1961,"
The 1961 Hawaiian Village Open Class.

"We are creating tomorrow now. There is no tomorrow that is going to come to us from outside somewhere; there is no tomorrow that can sneak up on us. . . . Tomorrow is an extension of our consciousness at this moment, and a divine grace or truth received in our consciousness now will externalize itself in some moment of what we might call the future, but which is not the future: it is but an extension of *now*. . . .

"God does not work in the future. God works only in the *now*. Think now of what is being prepared in the bushes and trees in our gardens. Think of what is being prepared now that will appear in May and June. . . . The activity of God in the *now*, now brings forth in May and June the flowers and the fruits. Think only that the activity of God must be working in the now. The activity of God is not going to bring us any fruits yesterday. God does not function in the past; the Christ does not function in the past or in the future: It is functioning now. . . . Your recognition of the activity of the Christ in you now is that which will appear as the fruitage in your life next week, next month, next season, next year. . . .

"There is no such thing as a past, but every moment of your present is a continuing experience into what the calendar calls the future. There is no such thing as one day ending and another day beginning. Those are just divisions that we make on calendars, but those of you who have been up until midnight some nights can bear witness to the fact that there is no division at midnight, no division at twelve o'clock noon: it is just the same rhythm taking place all the time, and it is always now."

Joel S. Goldsmith, "The Now Activity of the Christ," *The 1962 Glendale Open Class.*

Chapter Two

The Meaning of
Living Spiritually

In *The Thunder of Silence*[1] the incident of the baggage that was lost when I arrived in Johannesburg is recounted. The baggage had disappeared somewhere between my boarding the plane and disembarking and was not found for three weeks.

An experience such as this sometimes raises questions in the minds of students. Why is it that very successful practitioners and spiritual teachers sometimes still have problems, even serious problems? It seems to be the belief of many students that as soon as a person has attained a healing or teaching consciousness the trials and tribulations of this world are immediately ended. That is not true.

Humanhood Externalizes

As long as there is a trace of humanhood in a person, it will externalize itself as a human condition. A person could be ninety-nine percent spiritual and there would still be one per cent of humanness showing forth in his experience. But that is only one part and perhaps the lesser part of the story.

The greater part is this. As a rule, if those persons who are on the spiritual path reach the stage of healer and teacher, they have usually overcome ninety-five or ninety-eight percent, if not ninety-nine percent, of the world's discords. For them there will probably be no more discords, surely no more discords of any really serious nature. But regardless of the degree of demonstration of the practitioner or teacher, as long as he has a family, he will be involved in problems that arise from and through his family.

Should a practitioner by divine grace be able to rise above all the problems of family life, he may then begin to take on the problems of patients and students, and many a headache will come to him from his spiritual ministry. If he feels that he is being crucified, it will be because of his activity in the spiritual field. Nothing arouses the antagonism of the human mind quite as much as the things of the Spirit. The moment spiritual sense rises up, the whole world, or so it seems, tries to pull it down. Sad to say, this comes often through one's own students, not that it is always intentional, but even if it is not intentional, the results are the same.

In the Master's life his experience with Judas, Thomas, and Peter brought sadness and trouble to him. As a matter of fact, before his mission was completed, his disciples deserted him. None of them stood fast.

These experiences come to all alike. They come to those who are engaged in the spiritual ministry, but they also arise in the experience of students. They should not be taken too seriously, however, because no lasting harm will come of them. These problems serve as opportunities to further the spiritual development of the student.

It has been said that the last enemy to be overcome will be death. I do not know about that being the last enemy. Sometimes it seems that health and wealth are our greatest enemies. At least they are the greatest enemies to spiritual development. The moment health and a measure of supply come to us, we seem to be so delighted that we rest back and enjoy them, forgetting that until we make the transition from the physical sense of health to the spiritual or from the material sense of supply to the spiritual, we shall always be in the position of possibly having another ill come upon us at a future time.

Our greatest enemy is whatever enables us to sit back and rest as if now we are all right. We are never all right as long as an abundance of funds means supply. It is only when we have perceived the nature of that which produces health and supply that we can rest back because then we have achieved the ascension or a readiness for it.

The Infinite Way Reveals Universal Principles

The Infinite Way is a presentation of the mystical way of life, which is a way of life lived through conscious union with God. It makes no demands upon any person. It merely shows him how to live in attunement or at-one-ment with the principles of spiritual living. What an individual does with them is strictly his own affair.

The principles are not new. Infinite Way books are copyrighted not because the subject matter is new but because publishing houses protect their business investment by means of the copyright. But they are not copyrighted in the sense that I claim the message as mine, because the principles that are revealed in the Infinite Way are the result of a spiritual unfoldment that took place within me through many years of inner spiritual experiences, and are found in the original message of all major teachings. Lao-Tzu of China, Buddha and Shankara of India, Jesus of Nazareth, and John of Patmos had the same experiences, not necessarily in the same form, but they all had revealed within them these same principles. So there is nothing new about them in that sense except that the ideas are expressed in the language of the twentieth century.

In essence, the message of the Infinite Way begins with the realization that the Word must become flesh. Consciousness appears as form. Our consciousness appears as the form of our daily life. In the degree that we are entertaining a material sense of this world, in that degree does our consciousness externalize itself in material form and in material limitation.

As our consciousness becomes imbued with spiritual light, our outer experience becomes spiritual, harmonious, and perfect. There is a dying daily to our material sense of existence, and a transforming or a renewing through the transformation or renewing of consciousness. The responsibility for harmonious living rests not with fate, God, or the devil: it rests directly with us. We alone are responsible for our daily existence, for its harmonies and discords, remembering always that the temptation to accept discords and inharmonies can appear to come to us through those with whom we associate.

Reaping Material Consciousness

Whatsoever a man soweth,
that shall he also reap.

For he that soweth to his flesh
shall of the flesh reap corruption;
but he that soweth to the Spirit
shall of the Spirit reap life everlasting.

Galatians 6:7,8

Upon this principle depends much of the harmony or inharmony that touches us. As human beings we believe wholeheartedly in the power of the external world. From infancy and childhood, pleasure is found in rattles, dolls, trains, and guns, and as we grow older in real guns. We are taught to look outside ourselves for our good, either to a God up in heaven somewhere or to mama or papa, and then to each other. We look to business, to money, pills, powders, and bombs, always seeking our safety, security, peace, and health in the external world. That is the material state of consciousness. Those who continue to live in that state of consciousness continue to have the upward experience of good and the downward experience of sin, disease, death, lack, and limitation.

There are periods of good and there are periods of evil, periods of sickness and periods of health, but when all the experiences of the allotted threescore years and ten are added together, usually most persons testify to more discordant years, many more of them, than were completely healthful and harmonious. This is due to the materialistic state of consciousness which believes in the power of something or somebody outside one's own being.

Reaping Spiritual Consciousness

The spiritual state of consciousness has learned that the world of outer effect is not power, that all power comes from God, and that that power is made evident and manifests as what we call this external world. "The heavens declare the glory of God; and the firmament showeth his handywork."[2] We do not, therefore, do away with the heavens or the earth but realize that in and of themselves they are nothing except insofar as they show forth God's glory. That is true of you and of me, too.

In the spiritual way of life we come ultimately to the realization that "I can of mine own self do nothing."[3] I can of mine own self be nothing, and if I speak of myself I bear witness to a lie. It is only that the glory of God may be made visible and evident through my daily experience, in the health of my body and the wealth or fullness of my purse. Then when I have health or when I have an abundant supply, it is not really I, myself, who have done this thing or brought it about: it is that the health and the supply are God's glory being made manifest in my individual experience.

God is Spirit, and Spirit is invisible. Therefore, God can never be seen; God can never be heard, tasted, touched, or smelled through the physical senses. God is completely invisible.

When we recognize that, we then recognize that all the power in this world is in the Invisible. From the moment we recognize that truth, we lose all fear, hatred, and all undue love for anything in the external realm. Therein lies our safety, security, and peace.

"Yet have I not seen the righteous forsaken, nor his seed begging bread."[4] The righteous are those who know that the Invisible is the source of the visible and that faith and hope must forever be placed in the Invisible even though for the time being we cannot know what that Invisible is. Later, in periods of spiritual illumination, as we come face to face with that Invisible, we can see It, hear It, taste It, touch It, and smell It. The soul-faculties are cognizant of God at every level, and they are as much in individual communion with God as we are with someone near and dear to us. It is possible to be as friendly with God as we can be with one another. It is as possible to be on speaking terms with God as it is with one another. On the other hand, it is possible to be so silent that not even a word or thought escapes us, and yet be in constant communion with God.

"The place whereon thou standest is holy ground.[5]. . . The kingdom of God is within you.[6]. . . Son, thou art ever with me, and all that I have is thine."[7] The moment we begin, even in a slight measure, to perceive the truth of these statements, we never think of attaining anything outside of the radius of our own being. We begin then to realize that nothing can be added to us. In that lies the destruction of material sense. When a person perceives that nothing can be added to him, there is no need to desire anything, no need to want anything, no need to demonstrate anything, no need to do anything but stand still in the realization that the kingdom is already fulfilled within him.

Good Flows Forth From Consciousness

Let us assume that we have a problem of health, companionship, supply, or home. The first question we must ask ourselves is: Where will I find these things? The answer has to come back: within. These things do not exist external to our own consciousness; they cannot come to us. As I have explained before, if we had a fruit tree in our garden and we hung a ton of fruit on it, we would not have added to the supply of the tree. Supply does not come to trees that way, and the ton of fruit that we hang on it does not belong to the tree even after we have hung it there. The only thing that belongs to the tree is the fruit that comes from within and appears without.

Scripture tells us, "Cast thy bread upon the waters: for thou shalt find it after many days."[8] Another way of saying the same thing is that the kingdom of God is within us. Therefore, whatever we are seeking in life, we must stop seeking for and come into the agreement that it already exists within our own being. Then, as in the experience of the widow with the cruse of oil, the cruse never runs dry, even though in the beginning our material sense perceives that we have only a few drops.[9] But the cruse of oil did not fail. A spiritual master sees what the materialist can never see, and that is the infinite unfailing source of supply once we begin to let it flow.

This is true of every area of our experience. It is true of forgiveness. Let nobody expect forgiveness, because there is no God to give it to him. Forgiveness has to come from within a person's own being, and then it comes back to him. "Forgive us our debts, as we forgive our debtors."[10] There it is clear as a bell for everyone to see, to read, to hear. Our debts, or our sins, are forgiven in proportion as we learn to forgive.

Do we need companionship? We cannot get it. There is no way under the sun to demonstrate companionship, because it does not exist anywhere except within you and me. But when we begin to express companionship, we find companionship on every level of life. If we were abandoned on a desert island, it might be necessary to express companionship with clams, oysters, and egg shells or whatever we find around on that island—trees or coconuts. We have to share companionship with whatever is there until that flow of companionship from within us results in somebody else being washed up on the same island.

What Is Our True Identity?

Let us understand clearly that nothing can be added to us. Do we know our true identity? Do we know who we are? For therein lies the secret. Are we human beings? Are we sinners? Are we mortal? Is that our identity or is that a mistaken concept of ourselves which we must outgrow, outlive, and outlearn?

The truth of being is that in our innate purity we are sons of God. "The Spirit itself beareth witness with our spirit, that we are the children of God: And if children, then heirs; heirs of God, and joint-heirs with Christ"[11] to all the heavenly riches. In understanding our identity as children of God, God becomes the measure of our capacity, not that we of ourselves are anything, but that we are that place through which the infinite nature of God is pouring itself. This comes through the understanding of our true identity.

No place in scripture does Jesus Christ ask anything for himself. He feeds the multitudes; he heals the multitudes; he multiplies loaves and fishes; he finds gold in the fish's mouth; but at no time does he ask God for these. No, he lifted his eyes, and within him was the power of multiplication because he is the son of God. But so are you.

We are told distinctly that we are to "call no man your father upon the earth: for one is your Father, which is in heaven."[12] This being true, and God being our Father, our creative principle, as children of God we already have an infinity of good. It is embodied within us. It was placed there in the beginning "before Abraham was."[13] Before ever time began, God fulfilled Itself as the son. God the Father and God the son are one. God the Father fulfilled Himself as God the son, and you and I are that son. We are now fulfilled in our Christhood. How do we demonstrate that in our humanhood? First of all, by knowing this truth, by recognizing it, by acting on it, by never again looking outside ourselves for any form of demonstration, by trusting the within to appear in the without.

The secret of all being lies in the recognition of our true identity. If God is the Father and God is the son, then truly the son has all that the Father has, for the son and the Father are one. God is God the Father; God is God the son; and in that relationship of oneness everything is combined.

With that understanding, we are called upon to take the next step. "For he that hath, to him shall be given: and he that hath not, from him shall be taken even that which he hath."[14] Sounds like a very cold and cruel statement, but it happens to be spiritual truth, and whether or not we like it, we demonstrate this truth. When we understandingly realize that God constitutes our identity and that the kingdom of God is within us, from that moment on we no longer declare: "I have not; I need; I require; I desire; I wish; I want." Rather do we live in the consciousness that all that the Father has is ours, here, now, forever.

Do appearances always testify to that? No, if they did, there would never have been need for a metaphysical teaching or a spiritual one: we would be living it. But because of the sense of separation from God, we are not living as if God were the Father and the son. We are living as if God were in the sky somewhere and we poor mortals down on earth could not even get near It.

Why Demonstrations Are Lost

So through truth-teachings, we come back to a realization of our true identity. Then we live out from that realization, and having given up all desire and all attempts to demonstrate on the outer plane, the final truth is revealed to us. It is on this point that many metaphysicians have either lost or delayed their demonstration. I give it as my personal experience that the major stumbling block to harmony is that students are attempting to demonstrate health, supply, home, companionship, or some form of good. It can never be done. It has happened a few times accidentally; it has been done a few times through hypnotic suggestion; but it has never been accomplished as a spiritual demonstration because that would be violating God. If we could demonstrate supply or health, we would be violating every law that God has ever laid down for us.

There is only one demonstration that can result in permanent harmony for us, and that is the demonstration of God's presence. There is no other demonstration that can be made that is not just a magician's trick. God is all that we can demonstrate. The realization of the presence of God is all that we can demonstrate. When we demonstrate that consciousness we have it all because God constitutes all.

There is no such thing as real health separate and apart from God: God Itself is the health of our countenance. There is no such thing as supply separate and apart from God: God is the only supply there is on earth, God is all the supply there is, and there is no other supply. If we cannot demonstrate God, we cannot demonstrate supply. If we cannot demonstrate God, we cannot demonstrate the health of our countenance. There is no safety, there is no security, and there is no peace that can be demonstrated apart from God. God is the high tower; God is the fortress; therefore, God is the only safety.

God is the abiding place; therefore, God is the only home. We cannot demonstrate any other home. God is the only home; God is the abiding place, and if we do not abide in God and let God abide in us, we are as a branch that is cut off and withers. We have to abide in God, not in stone and wood. We have to demonstrate God, not stone and wood.

God is meat: *I* am the meat; *I* am the wine; *I* am the water; *I* am the bread of life. Therefore, we cannot demonstrate wine, water, bread, or meat. We demonstrate God and find that God is the meat, wine, water, and bread. Therein has been the failure of so many. They have left God out of the picture in order to demonstrate supply, happiness, safety, security, or peace of mind. It cannot be done. God is the only peace; God is the only mind; God is the only safety, the only security; God is the high tower, the fortress, and the abiding place.

"Thou art my hiding place; thou shalt preserve me from trouble.[15]. . . Thou art my hiding place and my shield."[16] God is all these things. How then can we pray for a hiding place? How can we pray for meat or wine or water when God is the meat, the wine, the water? This truth has been given us by the one we consider the Master. Yet we ignore his statement that we must not seek after what we shall eat or what we shall drink or wherewithal we shall be clothed.[17]

The Infinite Way has been built around the promise of the Master that the only thing that can be demonstrated is God, the realization of God, the conscious awareness of God, the consciousness of the presence of God, the hearing of the "still small voice,"[18] whatever term we wish to use for it. But until we are ready to give up all things—health, happiness, supply, safety, and security—and seek only this realization of God, we cannot come into the abundance of health, harmony, wholeness, completeness, and perfection, because they are not to be found outside of or apart from God.

Only One Demonstration Necessary

Many persons think in terms of using Truth and thereby cheat themselves. God cannot be used; Truth cannot be used. God can use us, if we are willing. Truth can use us, and when It does, It fulfills us and provides all things for us.

When we think in terms of using God or using Truth, we have to ask ourselves: Why am I using God or Truth? To get something or to get somebody? And so we have a something or a somebody separate from God. We cannot do it; we cannot violate God. When we have God we have all. It has been written that if we had God and the whole world, we would have no more than if we had God alone. If we ever had God, we would never give a thought to anything else. If right now we had God sitting beside us, what would we fear? Neither person, place, thing, nor devil. No, if we had the assurance of God's presence we would give up all thought of person, place, thing, or demonstration. We would say, "I've made my demonstration," and we would have, as soon as we had demonstrated a realization of God.

The basic premise of the message of the Infinite Way is to demonstrate God, demonstrate the realization of God, demonstrate the consciousness of God's presence, demonstrate the spiritual nature of God, demonstrate that mind "which was also in Christ Jesus."[19] Then we can forget all else because our sins will be forgiven, our diseases will be wiped out, our lacks will disappear, and the harmonies and grace of God will flood us.

It is not enough to tell a person to demonstrate the consciousness of God, because that leaves him exactly where he is now, feeling that he would love to do that if he knew how. So the Infinite Way writings and Infinite Way recordings are devoted to leading us to the point of demonstration. They show us how to keep our consciousness filled with the letter of truth, and how to take it in with our eye and how to take it in with our ear, so that it develops into the realization or spirit of truth. It is a rewarding experience to read truth, it is even more rewarding to hear it, and still more so when we can both read and hear it.

God Gives the Meditation or Treatment

When we read truth and hear truth and then make an effort to put into practice what we have read and heard, then what follows is an actual consciousness or experience of God's presence.

If we have practiced spiritual healing in our home, among our friends, or professionally, our success multiplies when we have known the truth consciously, that is, declared it, thought it, or read it. Instead of thinking that that constitutes the treatment or meditation, we realize that we have not even begun. We

have merely prepared ourself for the real treatment or meditation. It is the period following our knowing the truth in which
the meditation takes place. It is God that meditates and it is we
who receive it. "The word of God is quick, and powerful, and
sharper than any two-edged sword."[20] It says nothing about your
word or mine being sharp and powerful.

The Master very clearly says, "I can of mine own self do
nothing." So all the words and thoughts that we repeat have no
effect whatsoever on the problem or on the condition. The
effect is to lift us into a higher atmosphere where fear and concern disappear and we are then ready to enter that silence which
is meditation. We are ready to listen for the "still small voice" to
receive the inner assurance of God's grace. Then the healing
takes place, harmony appears, employment is found, supply, the
overcoming or the forgiveness of sin.

It is not you or I as human beings who can forgive sin. It is
not you or I who can ever counsel or give advice to anybody on
his human problems. But we can be still and we can let the
inner assurance of divine grace come, and then it will bring the
advice or counsel needed, the guidance and direction. It will
bring healing, harmony, and whatever form of good may be
necessary at the moment.

For too long, too many people have depended on their
treatments for healing work and found that their healing works
are far from certain. They never can be certain whether there is
going to be any result from them or what is going to happen.
This is because experience has proved to them that their treatments are not too effective, but they have not yet realized why.
A treatment that we give, a declaration of truth orally or silently is not for the sake of the healing: it is for your sake or mine,
to lift us into an altitude of consciousness wherein we can listen
for the "still small voice" and receive an inner assurance that
God is on the field, that Grace has taken over, that the divine
presence is there. Then we can know that healing has begun,
and sometimes has completed itself.

The Fruitage Spiritual Healing Brings

Healings can be instantaneous, although not always. If there has not been an enrichment of consciousness, if there has not been a greater degree or desire for spiritual things and the person is left only with a healthy body, he has not been saved from another experience and probably a worse one. For that reason it is not always desirable that a person have an instantaneous healing, because it leaves him free to go back to his old way of living, thinking, and being, with no benefit from the experience of the problem.

Every problem should result in a greater degree of understanding. Every problem should lift a person into a higher atmosphere of God. So it is we must never lose the regenerative effect a problem can have just by having it solved and then forgetting it.

Bearing Witness to God

We are called upon to make a transition through the acceptance of our divine sonship:

> I am not a human being; I am not a mortal;
> I am not at the mercy of time and tide;
> I am not at the mercy of material law.
> I was not created to be thus buffeted about.
>
> "I and my Father are one."[21]
> I was created in the image and likeness of God,
> the very presence of God,
> the very manifestation of God's being.
> In my true identity God constitutes my being.
> All that God is I am; and all that
> the Father has is mine.

Taking our stand as the spiritual son of God, we cannot go back to the old ways of seeking a demonstration. We have to stand fast in the realization: all demonstration is completed is us by virtue of our sonship. And then be patient enough to let it unfold.

There is a process that helps us in this. When we awaken in the morning and notice daylight as we look out the window, it is not too difficult to realize that all this happened while we were sleeping. Something must have been going on to turn that night into day, so we can acknowledge:

This is God's day.
God brought this day into being.
God changed the night into day.
God brought the light to us, the sun in the sky.
This day is God's handiwork.
This day belongs to God, and I belong to God, too.
So I see God at work turning night into day.

It is not difficult to notice the development of the flowers in our garden from day to day, and realize:

I did not bring these plants into being
or cause them to grow.
The life-force did it.
An invisible power is operating
in these plants bringing them
to fuller and fuller maturity.
Strange that I do not have to give them
a treatment to grow.
Strange that I do not have to pray for them.
Each day these plants are maturing more
and more, bringing forth flowers and fruit.
There is something going on
within them bringing all this about.

There is something going on
within me too,
bringing about my maturity,
turning the barrenness of the branch
I am into an abundance of fruitage.
I did not bring this about.
Something within, an invisible presence
and an invisible power functioning,
is bringing me to maturity,
to the fullness of life.
Since I can trust You, God,
to turn night into day, buds into blossoms,
so I can trust You with the whole of this day.
I turn this day over to You.
Furthermore, I am going to do
everything that is given me to do,
knowing that You have given it to me
to do and that You are helping me
in the fulfillment of it.

Living as a Beholder

The whole of our experience has to do with an acknowledgment that there is a God at hand; there is a God available; there is a God whose will is good; there is a God who does not give and who does not withhold, God who is a continuous state of activity appearing to us progressively. With our reliance on the infinite invisible, we are able to face any hour of the day knowing that God brought us to this hour.

As we awaken in the morning with the realization that God brought the morning to us and God has a fulfillment during this day for us, we are placing our life, our soul, our body, our business, our whole day in God's hands, and we are becoming God in action. Just as we behold dawn breaking into daylight, as we behold the stars coming out at night, just as we behold the activity in our garden, so do we become a beholder of our business or our family life in the realization that God it is that is doing it all, and that we are but the onlooker, the beholder, the beneficiary, the instrument.

Such a practice leads to an experience in meditation. All that has preceded this has been a contemplation which leads us to an introspective state of thought in which we become receptive to God within us. In one of those moments we make the actual contact with God, and God then begins to live our life. From then on the truth we have read about becomes our experience. Now we no longer have to think about it: we live it. And yet we are not really living it, but as Paul says, "Christ liveth in me."[22] There is an invisible something acting in us and through us without our taking conscious thought.

Thus we rise, not merely above the physical plane of life, but also above the mental plane into the spiritual, where we have no thought to take for anything. We have only to open our mouth, and God puts the words in. We have only to accept whatever obligations, duties, or responsibilities come to us, and God fulfills them through us. We are living the mystical life. We are living in conscious union with God.

God Brings Us the Work of Each Day

As long as the wheels of the mind are going around, planning and plotting, it is not spiritual living: it is mental living and it is a life of effort and very often a life of trial. When, through the contemplation and beholding of God, we come into an inner stillness, from that moment on there is no thought-taking or planning in life. Each day that we awaken we are given something to do, if not early in the morning, a little later in the morning, afternoon, or evening.

Many who achieve this degree of spiritual living find that it is not possible to stop there, and their meditations become deeper. Their ability to rest in communion with the Father deepens, and with that come greater revelations. With every revelation comes a responsibility. Nobody is ever given a revelation for his own good or for his own benefit. Nobody is ever given the knowledge of God merely for the solving of his personal problems. No one has ever received the grace of God for the purpose of using it for his own benefit. As a matter of fact, as soon as a depth of realization comes, all concern for one's personal self or life disappears, and then life begins to be lived on a universal plane. Life then is lived for whoever may be drawn to those who have received the vision, so that the world itself may be lifted up into a higher awareness.

Chapter Three

The Nature of the Messiah

The unfoldment of the activity of the Infinite Way is a testimony to the validity of the principles it sets forth. To begin with, here was a man in California who wrote a book presumed to be just a little pocket companion for himself and a few friends. He decided that a thousand copies would be more than enough for all persons, but the publisher pointed out that two thousand copies would cost very little more than one thousand, so two thousand were run off. I thought, of course, that we would have to have a great deal of storage space to take care of the second thousand.

Never did the idea occur to me that this message would travel around the world or that it would be of interest to anybody except the small group of patients and students who were around me. Furthermore, at that time there was no money for any kind of promotional activity; there were no "angels" to provide financial help; there was no organization, which there still is not; and there was no thought of my going any further than Los Angeles, California, with the message. No one was more surprised than I when someone invited me to give lectures in San Francisco, four hundred miles away. I thought, "What! Way up there they want to hear about this! That is strange, but it is beautiful because I would enjoy spending a week in San Francisco." I thought that that, too, would surely be the end of this activity.

And what has happened to the Infinite Way since those early days? It was first carried across the United States and Canada. Then a letter came from an important publisher in London, asking if he could publish a British edition of *The Infinite Way.* Could he? Why, that is a dream! Many American writers had been unable to have their books published in England after the war because of the scarcity of paper. Yet here was a firm asking, "May we?" That was not the end of it. Another firm in England asked to publish my books, followed by a request from Holland, and then Switzerland. This is a testimony bearing witness to the activity of God operating by Itself, financing Itself, publishing Itself, carrying Itself without a human being lifting a finger toward that end.

A Cardinal Principle of the Infinite Way

Never did I dream that there would be enough people interested in the message to warrant my going to South Africa. Then out of the blue came a letter asking me to stop off in South Africa on my trip to England and the Continent. Planes go by there every day, so it would be just a matter of having a couple of thousand dollars for an airplane ticket and a couple more thousand dollars for traveling expenses. With all of that, I saw more of a miracle than the students who were there to greet me saw.

The miracle was that the students in South Africa did not know me, and I did not know them. Yet when I arrived, there they were. If it were an activity of God that put me in South Africa, it would have to be for a purpose, and that purpose would not be mine or the students. That purpose would be God's purpose. If I had found myself in South Africa accidentally or through personal desire, then that whole visit would have been meaningless.

If it were an activity of God operating in the consciousness of those who were instrumental in humanly arranging my first trip to South Africa and if it were true that the activity of God in my consciousness took me 16,000 miles away from home, then that activity of God would have to be intended for some special benefit to those who came. When students begin to see this, they will understand a major principle of the Infinite Way, which is that God is fulfilling Itself, fulfilling Its plan as individual experience. We are not fulfilling God. God is fulfilling Itself through us as instruments of Its activity.

The Unpredictability of Human Experience

God does not function in the human scene. If God functioned in the human scene, there would not be a sin, a disease, or a death. There would not be a hospital or a mental institution if God were in the scene. The omnipotence, the omnipresence, and the omniscience of God preclude the possibility of any form of discord being present.

Human life is not under God guidance. When we rise above the human scene and our consciousness expands to an acceptance, a receptivity, and a responsiveness to the activity of God, then we are no longer human beings: we are the sons of God, spiritually fed, spiritually housed, spiritually clothed, spiritually governed. "I live; yet not I, but Christ liveth in me"[1]—but not as a human being. If Christ were living the life of human beings, they would certainly not be bombed out of any place, nor would they be in sin or discord of any nature. Where God is in operation, there is harmony.

Scripture makes it very clear that God gives us the power to become the sons of God, and it even explains when. "But as many as received him, to them gave he power to become the sons of God."[2] As human beings, we are the Prodigal Son, the son of a king, heir to a whole kingdom, who wandered away and wasted his substance and eventually found himself eating husks with the swine. That is what has happened to many of us. Some here may not have reached the end of the road where they have to eat husks with the swine, but if they should keep on their human way, they would eventually reach that point.

The Awakening

The discords of this earth are here because, like the Prodigal Son, we have wandered away from the Father's house and have become mortal beings. At some place in our wandering as the prodigal, the thought comes to us, "This is all wrong. This shouldn't be. Why am I in this plight? Why am I suffering this sin, disease, or lack? Why is my family undergoing such trials and tribulations? Why and why and why? There must be something wrong, and yet I am not that evil a man or woman that this kind of punishment should be visited on me or my family. Why? Why?"

Then one day something happens. Sometimes it happens without any outside aid as an experience in our own consciousness; sometimes someone hands us a book or tells us about a teaching or a teacher. We begin searching until we come to the realization that there is a spiritual way of life. It is a way that is not easy. Few there be that enter. But it is a sure way, and it is a way to harmony, peace, and wholeness. And we embark on that path.

It may be that we enter this path through one, two, or three of the many movements that are afoot or abroad today. There are many such paths that do lead to ultimate spiritual realization, and each person finds the one that suits his state of consciousness at the moment. If his interest is great enough, he progresses.

There is a danger in the early stages of this path. The danger is that we may get what we are looking for. If we do, it may keep us from getting what we should get, because when we first come to this path, we are looking primarily for health, supply, employment, companionship, or a better home. Many persons achieve these things and thereby lose their demonstration. When we find some measure of human improvement, we are all too apt to sit back and feel, "Isn't that wonderful? I can have everything I want just by a treatment or through my practitioner. I just call my practitioner and in an hour, it is all heaven." Thus we are tempted to rest back in that human sense of good and thereby very often fail to achieve our spiritual harmony.

The Hebrews Awaited the Fulfillment of Prophecy

The Hebrews had many farseeing prophets who led them into deep realizations, but evidently they were not able to hold onto them. After each prophet had come and gone, they slipped back into more and more difficulty until some prophet with deeper vision than most prophesied the coming of the Messiah, and from that day on, the Hebrews had a reason for living. They had a purpose and that was to await the coming of the Messiah.

The Messiah was to set the Hebrews free. At different periods, they wanted to be set free from different people and conditions, but always the Messiah was going to set them free from some thing or some person. The Messiah was to set up a new kingdom, and the Hebrews accepted that prophecy in its literal human sense. They, therefore, thought that the Messiah would be not only a religious leader, but a general to lead their armies against the enemies. After that he would establish them in prosperity.

They misunderstood the meaning of the Messiah because they interpreted It as a man who through a physical act would create a material kingdom. When the Messiah came, that is, when the Christ was revealed by the Master Christ Jesus, he did not put on a sword or lead them against Rome. He did not even take them out into the wilderness to set up a new kingdom or a new community. Instead, he kept them right where they were and tried to reveal the spiritual kingdom that was in their very midst, which would eventually set them free.

Jesus Preached a Kingdom Not of This World

The Master was actually a member of an underground spiritual order called the Essenes whose activities were directed against the Hebrew church. It was for that reason that the Hebrew church persecuted and drove them underground, and the Master was crucified, which was the penalty for insubordination against the church. The charge they made against him to the Roman authorities was that he was going to set up another kingdom, but the kingdom of which he taught was not of this world. They could not understand that. To them a kingdom meant so many square miles of land with a dictator or a king at its head. Since this was not the kind of kingdom he proposed, they turned on him and convinced Pilate that the Roman Empire was in danger from this man, and then they crucified him.

Rome had the legal right to crucify Jesus because of the charge made against him that he was plotting to set up another kingdom. He was. He was plotting to set up another kingdom in individual consciousness, in your consciousness and mine. That is what the Hebrews could not understand and that is why the Hebrews who did not become Christians remained Hebrews. The Hebrews who became Christians were those who began to realize the nature of a "house not made with hands, eternal in the heavens, [3] . . . the holy city, new Jerusalem." [4] Eyes cannot see, ears cannot hear, fingers cannot touch, nostrils cannot smell the new Jerusalem, that new kingdom which has its locale within us. That is where it is. It is never found outside: it is always within us.

Discouragement, the Tempter

The kingdom of God, preached by the Master, was well understood by a few of his disciples, although at the time of the crucifixion even they momentarily lost their vision for the same reason that we sometimes lose our vision. A person may have been a student of truth for many years, or he may know someone who has become a very successful practitioner or teacher, and then he sees that that practitioner or teacher is experiencing a sense of financial lack or some temporary sin or disease. Immediately the reaction of the student is that the principle does not work. Here is a person with a great understanding, and it has failed him.

That is what the Hebrews must have thought when they saw the Master on the cross: it does not work. Here was the man who could save others but could not save himself.[5] So they thought this man was not the promised Messiah. They did not realize that the presence of Jesus on the cross was the greatest spiritual demonstration that had ever been made up to that time, and probably unequaled to this day. They did not realize that his God had not failed him, but that his God was proving, through him, immortality, eternality, and that no matter what happened to the outer flesh, the inner kingdom was intact. Did he not say, "Destroy this temple, and in three days I will raise it up"[6]?

So, when a practitioner or teacher has an illness of some kind or encounters some other temptation or problem, even the practitioner or teacher may be tempted to believe, "I have wasted my life. This thing doesn't work. It isn't true. It isn't real. Why does this happen to me?"

Rising Above Human Good to Spiritual Reality

Students, even practitioners and teachers, do not realize that problems are their blessing, that God is showing them the difference between human health and spiritual eternality. Everyone must some day come to an end of human health and human wealth and make the transition into spiritual sonship in which never again can the laws of matter, the laws of economics, the laws of any material thing touch him. But there never will be a resurrection until there is a crucifixion; there never will be an ascension until there is a resurrection.

Unless we lose our life, we will never find our life eternal. That does not mean that we have to go through the torture that Jesus experienced on the cross; that does not mean that we have to be boiled in oil or die in prison. But it does mean that at some time or other some serious problem will force us to realize that physical harmony is not the solution to life, that physical freedom or the right to vote is not the solution to life's problems, nor is possessing a million dollars the solution. Then it is that we find the solution to be spiritual.

Health is not a matter of body: it is a matter of consciousness, and attaining that consciousness, we attain the health that is not at the mercy of matter, not even the nails on the cross. Nothing can destroy our life; nothing can destroy our body once we have the realization of Spirit; but we will not arrive at that state while we are sitting back comfortably with a healthy body, a loving family, and an abundance of supply, because it is so easy to rest back in a good human experience.

At some period or other, each one of us must come to the place where we realize that the nature of the Messiah is not merely to give us a heart, a liver, and lungs that function, or even to provide us with so many dollars a week. The function of the Messiah is to reveal to us our spiritual identity and the eternality and immortality of our being and body.

Immortality Revealed

"Yet in my flesh shall I see God."[7] Right now, here and now on earth, we must eventually meet our eternality and immortality face to face so that when the time comes for us to make the transition from the human scene, we do not get kicked out of the body: we walk out of it. We do not lie around for years suffering with disease, trying to get free of it, but we go to sleep some night and find that our work is finished on this plane, and with that realization comes a readiness to step out into the next plane. That realization must come to each one of us, just as each one of us has discovered that the concept of ourselves as a baby-body is no longer anywhere around. What happened to it? Did it die? No, we evolved out of that concept into the body of a child, and looking at our body now, we realize that we have evolved out of the body of childhood into maturity.

The only reason the body weakens and degenerates into the beliefs of old age is because we have accepted the material theory of disintegrating matter. We think that all matter must disintegrate and deteriorate at some time, so we are prepared to accept threescore years and ten as the probable limit to life. When we are thirty five, thirty eight, or forty and go to a doctor, we are told that we must expect the body to run down from now on. We must take different care of our body now than we did heretofore. We have all accepted that, and that is what we demonstrate.

The Purpose of the Messiah

When we understand correctly the nature of the Messiah, we will understand what the great Hebrew prophets who prophesied the coming of a Messiah understood Its purpose to be. Through meditation on that subject, an unfoldment will take place within us revealing that the purpose of the Messiah is to heal the sick and raise the dead. Why raise the dead? Because God has no pleasure in our dying whether we are the daughter of Jairus, a young child, or Peter's grandmother, an old lady. Regardless of age, we must be raised from the dead, because there is no plan in God's universe for death. There is only a plan for progressive unfoldment from childhood to maturity and from maturity into that phase of existence which may transcend our present concept of body and universe.

It is important for us to take into our meditation the place
the Messiah is to have in our experience. What part is It to play?
What is Its function? It is not enough as a Hebrew to prophesy
the coming of a Messiah; it is not enough as a Christian to say,
"Oh, Christ will come again." As truth-students, it is our function to realize:

> Christ, the Messiah, is within me.
> The son of God is the very essence of my being.
> But what is Its function?
> What is the Christ supposed to do within me?
> What is Its revelation?
> What is it that the Master Christ Jesus
> tried to tell the Hebrews that
> most of them could not accept
> and never saw? What is it?

When we discover the nature of the Christ we will begin to
see Its purpose in our experience. One thing that is delaying Its
realization is that as truth-students many of us believe that the
function of the Christ is to make our sick body well, to double
our income, to get us a better home or a better companion.
That is what we are waiting to have happen, but that is not the
function of the Christ.

The purpose of the Christ is not to improve our humanhood. The purpose of the Christ is to reveal our spiritual identity, to reveal that we are the children of God, eternal and
immortal now. That is quite different from believing that the
Christ is going to find a parking place for us.

Earth Is Heaven

This is a spiritual universe. How many of us have realized
that the laws of matter accepted in the mind of man as govern-

ing this world are not the real laws of this universe? It is because
we accept them as real that we pay the penalty for them. God is
spirit and God is infinite. So, the creation of God must be spiritual and infinite and the laws of God governing Its creation
must be spiritual.

As in heaven, so on earth. Whatever God is in heaven, that
is what God is on earth. Whatever heaven is in heaven, that is
what heaven is on earth. Why? There is no such thing as heav-
en *and* earth. There is a heaven appearing to us as our earth, but
when we look out at it, it does not seem that way to us. Because
we have failed to see this point, we have believed that when the
Christ comes to us, It is supposed to do material things for us.

The Master revealed the spiritual body and spiritual universe
to those of his day, but, even after having touched his enlightened consciousness, it is said that only about five hundred persons witnessed the resurrection. Out of all the multitudes that
Jesus healed and fed, only about five hundred were witnesses to
the truth that his body was spiritual and that it was not in a
tomb, and that no tomb could hold it. When we understand
that, no tomb will ever hold our body, any more than a tomb will
hold us. We are spirit, and our body is spiritual. It is governed by
spiritual law, spiritual substance, spiritual activity, spiritual wisdom, not the wisdom of man, but the wisdom of God.

Spirituality, the Fruitage of Sowing to the Spirit

The Master was very clear that as we sow so shall we reap.
Can we really believe that we can sow to the flesh and then reap
Christhood? No, not if Jesus the Christ were walking this earth,
not if Jesus the Christ were in this very room could those who
are sowing to the flesh reap spirituality. Spirituality cannot be
conferred on anyone any more than honesty or integrity or
morality can be conferred on him. That is something we have to
discover within our own being, just as Christhood cannot be
conferred on us except in proportion to our sowing to the Spirit.

Then, and then only, will we reap life everlasting.

It is possible for a teacher to come along and lift us so high out of human consciousness that never again will we wholly come down to earth. Never again will we be the same person. Let us not think, however, that there has ever lived a teacher or ever will be one who can do that *en masse* or for everybody sitting in a room.

Each one is weighting himself down by what he is sowing or he is readying himself for the Christ by sowing to the Spirit. When we are no longer expecting the Spirit to do material tricks for us, then the Master can come. The Christ can come in the form of a human teacher; the Christ can come in the form of a book that opens our consciousness to the spiritual experience, or the Christ can come without any human avenue or instrument or help.

The Christ can come to our individual consciousness, and will, without the help of a teacher or a book, if we begin to sow to the Spirit, if we begin to look on life as a spiritual experience and begin to conform to the ways of God. We cannot violate the laws of God and reap the blessings of God.

True, to the woman taken in adultery the Master said, "Neither do I condemn thee: go, and sin no more."[8] And I can assure you that she had no further penalty to pay. Is that strange? No, the Master saw that regardless of what she may have done outwardly, inwardly there was a drive toward God, and in recognizing the Christ of Jesus she made it possible for him to free her from the human sense of life.

It was the same with the thief on the cross, who was crucified. The very moment he turned to the Master, his past sin was wiped out, and the Master could promise, "To day shalt thou be with me in paradise."[9] So it is with us. Our sins or ignorance of yesterday cannot prevent our spiritual ascension today. There is not a long period of reformation; there is not a long period of sackcloth and ashes: there is only the period in which we awaken to the realization, "This is not what I want. *This* is what I want." In the moment when we come to the realization that this is the way we are going, the Master can say, "Good, the past has been wiped out."

Release the Past

Even if Jesus Christ were sitting here in our midst, however, the wiping out of the past cannot take place in the experience of anyone unless he has released yesterday. The thief on the cross released yesterday by crying out to the Master. The woman taken in adultery released the past when she looked up in the direction of the Master as much as to say, "Save me, save me." Save her from what? Being stoned? Oh no! She was asking to be saved from the beliefs that hampered her yesterday and kept her in the life she had been living.

Our work, too, is not primarily the healing of a sick body. If that were our only interest, we would withdraw from the healing work and students could turn to *materia medica*. On the whole *materia medica* is doing a good job on the physical plane. Those who do not receive their healing and pass on soon discover that they are not dead. So there cannot be too much concern about whether or not we have a well body. The well body must come to us as the result of the realization of our spiritual identity.

Many persons have remarkable healings through a practitioner's or teacher's work and then go right back to their human way of life. Nothing has happened to them. Just to make a sick body well is not the function of this work. Its function is to reveal the nature of the Messiah, the Christ, so that we may come into our spiritual life, our divine sonship. Then we not only have health, harmony, abundance, and all of the other good things of life, but we are able in a measure to impart truth to others.

A person with one grain of spiritual revelation, no matter how small, will begin at once to do some healing work. Every grain of spiritual realization we attain lifts this world higher, if it is but one step higher, out of its materiality. As we attain even one degree of spiritual awareness we are in that degree a light on this earth, although very often we do not even know that anyone benefits. We may not know the blessing that we are to those around us. I have witnessed this in my own work from my first spiritual experience and with students. They themselves have sometimes come to me and said, "You'll never be proud of me. I really know less now than when you first taught me."

And I would respond, "I like to hear that. That's a good student." Let no one ever come and tell me that he understands how healing comes about because then I will know that he is not a good student. I have never found a student who understood how healing is done. I don't understand it yet myself. But then with the students who did not feel they knew, the healing works began, and they would eagerly ask, "How does it happen? I really don't know. We don't have to know. One of these days it will be revealed to them that they are not healing anything, but that God, the very activity of the Christ, is revealing to them the spiritual sonship of somebody who looks like a human being, but who is in truth the Christ.

We have accepted what we see with the eyes and hear with the ears, even though we have been told, "Judge not according to the appearance, but judge righteous judgment."[10] Let no one believe for a moment that it makes any difference if he humanly looks at a person and says, "Oh, he's spiritual being." That would not heal even a headache. There is an actual spiritual vision, and when we have that vision we can look at a person and not see a human being. Instead we behold the son of God.

To look with our eyes and see a human being, while saying, "Oh, that's the Christ," is meaningless. Those are words, clouds without rain, a meaningless affirmation. The Master referred to it this way: "Having eyes, see ye not? and having ears, hear ye not?"[11] Yes, we have eyes and we have ears, but Jesus did not mean those eyes and those ears. He was talking about an inner vision which, when we have it, we know that we are not healing a disease: we are seeing that there is no disease out there. We are not declaring it; we are not affirming it: we are actually witnessing the truth that there is no disease; there is no mortal man. There is the difference. This is spiritual consciousness, Christ-consciousness, or the fourth dimension.

Human consciousness is the three-dimensional consciousness through which we can see height, weight, and depth. With the fourth dimension we see that which is invisible, we hear that which is inaudible, and we know that which is unknowable. It is an inner discernment of something that the eyes cannot see and the brain cannot even believe. Those of vision have always been able to see beyond the visible. For example, to the person of limited vision, Jules Verne's *Twenty Thousand Leagues Under the Sea* was a fairy tale, and the submarine something that could never come about. Leonardo da Vinci's airplane that would never fly was the foolishness of several centuries ago. These were impossibilities, but somebody came along with a different vision, and saw and heard what nobody else had ever seen or heard.

So it is in the spiritual realm. If we judge by eyesight, we are a group of human beings hoping to be rid of the discords and inharmonies of our humanhood and probably believing that we will be satisfied if we can experience some of the harmonies of humanhood. That is what the picture says, but that is not true. That is not why you are studying this letter, even if you do not know it. You have come to this message that your Christhood may be recognized and saluted. We turn to a teacher so that someone who can see with the eyes closed and can hear with the ears closed, who has an inner vision may look through our outer appearance, look through our sins, false appetites, false desires, lusts, and ambitions and see at the center of our being the son of God which is already there. Seeing, knowing, saluting, and greeting It brings It out into visible tangible manifestation and expression.

God is not in the human scene, or our physical human bodies would be immortal. But let us forget the human scene, recognize and realize the nature of the Christ. Let It reveal Itself as our spiritual identity, and then we will find that our bodies are immortal and that God is in that scene. That is the strange part! It is a paradox that in one breath God is not in the human scene and in the very next breath God is in the human scene. But that is the way it is.

TAPE RECORDED EXCERPTS
Prepared by the Editor

Within each of us is the power of resurrection. We do not have to seek afar for it because that power is embodied within us, and it becomes an experience of renewal and restoration as it is released from within. The excerpt below reveals the nature of this power of resurrection.

The Resurrecting Power of Love

"'I and my Father are one,' and in this oneness I find, not only spiritual power; I find my food, wine, water, inspiration, even resurrection. . . . Scripture reveals from beginning to end that there is a power that restores to us the lost years of the locust. There is a power of resurrection, a power of restoration, regeneration, and above all things, the Master came to reveal that this power is within you. He restored to full and complete dignity the woman taken in adultery; he restored to heaven the thief on the cross. This is all resurrection, restoration, regeneration. . . .

"The power of resurrection lies in love, and that is difficult. Everybody wants to be loved, and so few want to love. It is only in loving that resurrection can come. It is not in being loved. We could be loved by millions and still die miserably.

"The power of resurrection is not in the love that is given to us: the power of resurrection is in the love that flows through us, out from us. In other words, 'the imprisoned splendor' must be permitted to escape, and that imprisoned splendor is your life eternal, but life is love. There is no life separate and apart from love. . . .

"As you travel, you meet so many people who find life to be futile, who find that life is not really worthwhile; it is not all that it is cracked up to be. If you get to know them very well, you will see why. The power of love has left them, not the power of being loved. No, they are spending most of their life seeking love. . . and they never find it, because it is not to be found: it is to be expressed.

"So it is! If you want life, and I mean life harmonious, not just an existence from morning to night and night to morning, real life, a life abundant in every way—physically, mentally, morally, financially—you do not go around looking for life: you live; you live! . . . You cannot just keep on living unless you have something to live for. The moment a reason for living disappears, life disappears.

"The only reason there ever is for living is love. . . . There is no other reason for staying on earth than the opportunity to love. Anybody who has experienced this knows that there is no joy like loving, no joy like sharing, bestowing, understanding, giving. . . ."

Joel S. Goldsmith, "The Principle of Power and Love,"
The 1962 Princess Kaiulani Open Class.

Chapter Four

God Formed Man
for His Glory

But the natural man receiveth not
the things of the Spirit of God:
for they are foolishness unto him:
neither can he know them,
because they are spiritually discerned.

I Corinthians 2:14

If a spiritual message such as the Infinite Way sounds like foolishness to you, it is because you are seeing and hearing as a human being and can be counted among those of whom Jesus spoke, "Having eyes, see ye not? and having ears, hear ye not?"[1] If, on the other hand, this message makes sense to you, it is because your human sense of life is becoming fainter and your spiritual discernment is being awakened and aroused to perceive it. In a colloquy with his disciples the Master asked:

Whom do men say that I the Son of man am?

And they said, Some say that thou art
John the Baptist: some, Elias; and others, Jeremias,
or one of the prophets. . . .

But whom say ye that I am?

And Simon Peter answered and said,
Thou art the Christ, the Son of the living God.

And Jesus answered and said unto him,
Blessed art thou, Simon Barjona:
for flesh and blood hath not revealed it unto thee,
but my Father which is in heaven.
                                    Matthew 16:13-17

It was as if Jesus had said to the disciples: "The mind did not tell you that; your eyes did not see it; your ears did not hear it: the Father within you, your spiritual sense, revealed it to you." So it is with a spiritual message. You will never learn a spiritual message merely through the physical senses, not by seeing or by hearing. You will learn a spiritual message when your heavenly Father, that is, your spiritual consciousness, is awake and reveals to you that this is truth, this is the Christ, this is reality. Then are you able to accept it, receive it, respond to it, and demonstrate it.

Thought Is Not Power

Some persons have accepted the belief that their human mind is God and that by thinking good thoughts they will come true. There are some who believe that if you send them a good thought it will benefit them, or that if you send them a bad thought it might give them a headache or kill them. All utter nonsense! The thoughts of man are powerless. Whether a person sends you a good thought or a bad thought, it is still not power.

Mark Twain was very clear about this. On a trip to England he was taken sick on board ship, but when he landed in England, he was all right. Reporters who met him when the ship docked said, "Mr. Clemens, thousands of cables have come from the United States, telling us that all America has been praying for you during your illness."

Mark Twain's reply was, "That's nice. Will you send back word that I am sure it hasn't hurt me at all?"

If human prayers or human good thoughts were of any value, would parents ever lose a child? Would a child ever lose a parent? All of us are filled with good thoughts for our children and our parents. What good does it do? Children and parents become sick and die. Our work is to rise above the belief that a good thought is a blessing and a bad thought a curse. There is only one thing that is a blessing and a power, and that is a realization of the presence and power of God which comes with a conscious God-contact.

You could sit from now until doomsday and talk about the light you could have in a dark room from electricity and yet continue to be in darkness. Talking about the wonders of electricity and light will not do anything for you. You have to plug in the bulb, make the connection, and turn on the power. Then there is light. You can talk about God, think about God, do anything you like, and still be in darkness. It is only when you make your conscious contact that you experience God presence and power. It is not good thinking and it is not bad thinking that has a thing to do with it. What counts is God-realization, the actual experience of God.

There is no basis whatsoever for the belief that just because you think good thoughts about a person that will make good things come true. It is sad to see to what extent that has failed. It is even more sad that there are people who believe that other persons' wrong thinking can harm them. It is an abomination against God to believe that there is a power opposed to God, to believe that if you are living the life of the Spirit that evil is so powerful that it can overcome God's being.

Never fear what mortal man can do to you. Never fear the thoughts or the daggers of the assassin or the mental malpractitioner. "No weapon that is formed against thee shall prosper,"[2] unless you barb it or give it power by accepting a power apart from God. You're the one responsible for what you accept.

Holy Ground

All blessings take place in your individual consciousness. Even Jesus Christ could not bless you unless you opened yourself to that blessing. There is no person and there is no power great enough to bless you against your will or while you are in violation of God's will.

Open yourself to the realization that inside of you God has centered Its being, Its activity, Its presence, and Its power. "The place whereon thou standest is holy ground."[3] Right here where you are is holy ground. If you make your bed in hell, there is holy ground. If you walk through "the valley of the shadow of death"[4] there, too, is holy ground. No matter where you are, the fact of your being there makes it holy ground because wherever you are *I Am*. Why? Because I and the Father are one. In that oneness are the allness, the completeness, and the perfection of being, and when you are convinced of that truth, you will have learned one of the greatest secrets in the world. There is no power either for good or evil external to your own being.

Sooner or later, and it might just as well be sooner, this minute, you will have to agree that right where you are is the fullness of the Godhead bodily.

> Right here all that God is, I am.
> All that the Father has is mine.
> "Son, thou art ever with me,
> and all that I have is thine."[5]

If you recognize the truth that right here where you are is holy ground, right here are the presence, the power, the infinity, the allness, and the goodness of God, never again will you look outside for your good. Never again will you seek justice, kindness, recognition, or gratitude from another. Never again can you look outside yourself for anything.

You must always remember that it is only because the all-ness, the infinity of God, is here that you are in a position to share it. You can feed five thousand. You can heal the multitudes. It is not you as a person doing it. It is because where you are the Father is, and all that the Father has is yours. For what purpose? To lay up your treasure "where moth and rust doth corrupt"[6]? No, to share. If it is truth pouring through to you, it is God-truth pouring through, but it could just as well be food, money, or housing. It makes no difference. Anything can pour forth through you if you acknowledge: " 'I can of mine own self do nothing,'[7] but all that the Father has can flow through me."

All Good Flows Forth From Within

As you take the attitude that you are seeking nothing out here—no reward, no gratitude, no recognition, nothing—that you are willing that the allness of God pour through you, then your good is the reflex action of that awareness of omnipresence right here. Thus your good flows to you. It may come through some person close to you, or it may come through many other persons outside, but it is bound to come, because it is the bread you have cast upon the waters coming back with jam, marmalade, and sugar, or whatever other things you like on your toast.

"For he that hath, to him shall be given: and he that hath not, from him shall be taken even that which he hath."[8] That is a hard saying. But that is exactly what it means. If you will admit that "the earth is the Lord's, and the fulness thereof,"[9] and "Son, all that I have is thine," you can fulfill every demand that is made upon you. If you live in that awareness, then it will be literally true that the cruse of oil will never run dry; but not if you look out here and seek to draw something to you or if you pray to God to bring something to you. You will be separating yourself from your good every time you pray for it to come to you because there is nothing outside of consciousness.

The presence of God is infinite and fills all space. Therefore everything must flow out from within. When you take that position, you are beginning to perceive the nature of spiritual sonship. If you are a spiritual son of God, you are an heir of God and joint-heir to all the heavenly riches. How then would you dare look outside yourself? How can you call yourself a son of God in one breath and then expect something of somebody in the next breath? There is the mistake that is so often made. We keep saying that we are one with the Father and all that the Father has is ours, and then we begin praying for something more to be added to us. It cannot be done. There is the reason for failure.

The Function of the Christ

If you understand the nature of the Messiah that the Hebrews prophesied, or the nature of the Christ that many Christians are awaiting to reappear, you will realize, first of all, that It is not going to reappear, because there never was a time when It appeared. It has always been right within your own being awaiting your recognition. If you recognize the Christ to be the truth of your spiritual sonship, then look to It to multiply your loaves and fishes; look to It to heal the sick and to raise the dead; look to It to supply and to strengthen you; look to It to go out before you and "make the crooked places straight."[10] If the son of God has Its abiding place within you, then it is from within you that you must expect your good to flow.

Any prayer that some good can happen or come to you or that anything can be added to you is a waste of time and effort. All that the Father has is already yours. What more do you want? Only one thing more: the realization of that. You do not want to get happiness: you want the realization of the happiness that already is within you. You do not want to get supply: you want the realization of the spirit of God which is supply. You do not want health: you want a realization of the Christ at the center of your being.

John the Baptist in prison was beginning to fear that maybe Jesus was not the Messiah he had been telling about, so he sent two of his disciples to ask him, "Art thou he that should come, or do we look for another? Jesus answered and said unto them, Go and shew John again those things which ye do hear and see: The blind receive their sight, and the lame walk, the lepers are cleansed, and the deaf hear, the dead are raised up, and the poor have the gospel preached to them."[11] That is the function of the Christ: to heal sickness, raise the dead, feed the hungry, loose those in prison.

When is the Christ? Now! Where is the Christ? Within you! If you are to be healed, if you are to be fed, clothed, or housed, if you are to be raised from these dead and mortal beliefs, if you are to be given your spiritual freedom, it must come from within your own being. You must look to the Christ of your being to be the multiplier of loaves and fishes, to be that which is the activity revealing harmony in your experience. This can come only when you make the admission that the place whereon you stand is holy ground, that the spirit of God has said, "Son, *I* will never leave you. Son, thou art ever with me. Son, all that *I* have is thine in this very instant." In the recognition of that, you can give up all desire for your good to come from without, and then let it come in whatever natural way the unfoldment may take place.

The Signs Follow

You will be surprised at the way your good comes to you sometimes when you have given up all thought of the channels or instruments through which it should come, the time when it should come, or even what it is that should come, because it is literally true that "we know not what we should pray for as we ought."[12] You must let the Spirit bear intercession with your spirit and reveal to you what it is that you must have. When you say, "I know not how to go out or how to come in; I know not how to pray or what to pray for," you are beginning to touch the hem of the understanding of prayer.

All the words in this *Letter* are as meaningless as yesterday's newspaper except as they become a realization. Meditation is the way to realization. All the treatments or prayers spoken or thought, even when they are correct, are without power. Even good thoughts are without power. It is only after you have had your contemplative meditation and can rest back in meditation and wait for God to place the seal on it as an inner release that you can be assured that there will be signs following.

It says in scripture, "There shall no sign be given."[13] The "signs shall follow them that believe."[14] In other words, regardless of what you think or do not think, regardless of what you study or do not study, no sign will be given you. But the moment you attain a realization of the presence of God, from then on the signs follow.

In our work, meditation is of far more importance than any other activity. Meditation is entirely individual, although you can meditate in groups and benefit from it if there is one or more in that group who has attained some measure of the fourth dimensional consciousness. But the experience of meditation ultimately becomes an individual one. You, yourself, have to come to a place within you where a release comes, where there is an awareness of an inner contact. Then there are signs following: harmony, healings, and all good.

It is easier to meditate with someone of realized consciousness. You may have more difficulty in attaining meditation when you are alone. Then you will have to be patient with yourself after you have a contemplative meditation until you are able to abide in peace within yourself, feel a stirring, a deep breath, or a release, some kind of an awareness that assures you that God is on the field.

Confrontation and Argumentation, No Part of the Spiritual Life

Do not permit yourself to be drawn into discussion about your spiritual life, the wrongness or the rightness of it. Only God at the center of your being can tell you that. That is something that has to be decided within your own being. There are aspects of your life which are entirely individual, and the spiritual life is one of these. It must be lived alone. No one can live it for you. The Master said, "He that loveth father or mother more than me is not worthy of me."[15] I do not believe that Jesus meant that you were to desert them or abandon them, but as the spiritual life touches you, if it does not touch the members of your family, you must live it within yourself and let them live their life.

If the spiritual life touches you, but does not touch your business associates or social acquaintances, let them live their life and you live yours. Do not try to talk them out of their convictions or beliefs, but neither should you give them the opportunity to talk you out of your convictions and beliefs. The time must come when every spiritual decision will be made within yourself. The more spiritual every conviction becomes, the more antagonistic it will be to the human world. Only by keeping these things within yourself can you protect them.

The Hebrews thought they were going to save their religious institutions by fighting the Master, just as many churches have fought governments and each other because they feared what might happen to them. Today there are those who would fight you individually to save what they call their teachings or their entrenched institutions, not knowing that it is folly. If a thing is of God, there is no use fighting against it because God is going to prosper it. If it is of man there is no use fighting against it or arguing against it either; it is going to fall of its own nothingness.

You have no quarrel with anyone, but do not leave yourself

open to argue or quarrel with others. It is not that truth can be destroyed or that you can be destroyed, but until you are at that place where you can "walk on the water", it would be better for you to tell no man what things you believe.

You may talk it over with those of your own spiritual household, but be sure they are of your household. Share with those who are receptive and responsive to this word, but to the rest of the world a spiritual activity such as the Infinite Way exists really as a spiritual underground. Infinite Way students are not trying to use the world's weapons to save the world; they are not trying to proselyte or to draw the world to the Christ or to their way. Instead, they bear witness to what is within them and then let those who have eyes to see benefit from what they witness.

There are startling truths in spiritual wisdom, which the world cannot yet bear, some things which students themselves at times do not wish to face. One such revelation is that God never rewards you for being good, and God never punishes you for being evil. Most persons do not like that. But it is true. No longer look to God for your blessings or fear God in the sense of punishment, because none of those things comes from God.

Whatever good comes to you comes from your own sowing. That determines your reaping. Whatever of evil comes to you comes from your own inner acceptance of two powers, a power of good and a power of evil. If there is a power of evil, there is no use studying anymore, because if God could not overcome it, you cannot.

Infinite, Indivisible Individuality

"Know ye not that ye are the temple of God, and that the spirit of God dwelleth in you?"[16] You are that temple. Individually, you and I are the temple of the living God, and God must be in His holy temple now. The kingdom of God is within you, so that individually you are that place through which all of the Godhead flows.

This brings up a very important point. You and I are not parts of God because if we were it would take all of us to make up God. Then if one of us were absent a little piece of God would be missing. If somebody happened to die, a little bit of immortal life would disappear. That cannot be possible. God cannot be divided. God is not divisible any more than integrity is divisible, or morality, honesty, or loyalty. If you have these qualities, you have all of them, one hundred per cent of them. That does not bar me from having one hundred per cent of them also. It is like the sun in the sky. The sun is not divisible; we do not get a little piece of sun. The sun shines in its fullness, in its allness.

It is important to remember that God is not divisible and that you are not a little piece of God. If you cannot bring through in your individual experience one hundred per cent integrity there is something lacking in the whole scheme of life. If you cannot bring through one hundred per cent loyalty, fidelity, morality, goodness, or benevolence, you have nothing. A person who is ninety-nine per cent moral is not moral at all. A person who is ninety-nine per cent honest is not honest at all. There is either honesty, morality, integrity, loyalty, or there is not.

The fullness of the Godhead bodily projects itself as our individual experience so that when the Father says, "Son, all that I have is thine," He has not forgotten that He has other sons. The father of the Prodigal had two sons. To the one, he said, "All that I have is thine," but just before that he had given away a jeweled ring and a royal robe to the other son.

While materially you can divide up and portion out, spiritually that is an impossibility. Spiritually all that the Father has, which means all the wisdom, all the love, all the joy, all the peace, all the security, all the safety, all the allness of God, is individually yours and mine. That does not mean that you and I are now demonstrating that in its fullness. We are demonstrating God's allness to the degree of our developed state of consciousness.

There are states and stages of consciousness. It can be likened to music. Music cannot withhold any of itself from individual you and me. But there are some who have a greater capacity for letting music flow through them, others a lesser capacity, and some none at all. That has nothing to do with the allness of music, nor has it anything to do with our ability to bring through the allness of music. If we were to give the consecration and the devotion that a Paderewski had or a Caruso, perhaps some of us would bring through the same degree of music which they did.

The Master indicated that if the disciples had had just a little more understanding, a little more faith, they also would have healed the cases that they failed to heal and had to bring to him. The allness of spiritual power and presence is yours in proportion as you can open your consciousness to it. God has no ability to withhold anything from you. God is a state of eternal divine being. God always is and always is in Its fullness. God is the infinite all good. Nothing that would have the power to withhold good could be the infinite all good. God is love. That which would withhold your health, your safety, or security certainly could not be called love. God cannot withhold anything from you but you can block it; you can shut it off.

Greater Awareness Eliminates
the Consequences of Ignorance

"Whatsoever a man soweth, that shall he also reap."[17] If you are in disobedience to the laws of God, you shut yourself off from God's grace. It is the same as the sunshine. The sun cannot withhold itself from your home, but you can draw the shades in your home and keep it out. You can separate yourself from it. It is the prodigal state of consciousness that shuts itself off from God's love. Immediately as you turn to the Father's house, divine grace takes over.

It is like a problem in mathematics. If for ten years you

believed that two times two were five and in all of your business transactions you continued to give out five for four under that belief, all of the ten years you were paying a severe penalty for such faulty handling of your affairs. But as soon as it is brought to your attention that two times two is four, your penalty is wiped out. From then on your transactions are all correct, and there is no penalty for what you believed yesterday. Divine grace has wiped that out and today you begin again.

In the Oriental teaching karma is identical with the Master's as-ye-sow-so-shall-ye-reap. But the Judaic-Christian teachings, contrary to the Oriental, are very emphatic on the point that "though your sins be as scarlet, they shall be as white as snow."[18] Your karma is wiped out in the instant when you lift yourself above today's state of consciousness and enter the higher consciousness which is governed by Grace instead of by law. "The law was given by Moses"—and that means the law of good and evil, the law of cause and effect, the law of as-ye-sow-so-shall-ye-reap—"but grace and truth came by Jesus Christ."[19] Grace brings the instantaneous wiping out of all effects of the law.

Grace Sets Aside Material Law

You have undoubtedly witnessed some spiritual healings in your own experience or the experience of others. Perhaps someone has had a cold and has called upon a practitioner for help, and within a very short time found all the effects or symptoms of the cold gone. It may have been a fever, which without the use of any material remedy, disappeared a short while after the treatment was given.

Every healing that has ever taken place through spiritual means is a direct violation of law, brought forth through an activity of Grace. A fever is supposed to keep going up and up and up as long as the condition that caused it is there. Some external remedy must be introduced to bring down or wipe out that fever. That is the medical law. But along comes divine grace and without the application of material remedies, without any human means, and without the length of time that *materia medica* would claim is necessary, there is an instantaneous return to normalcy. Thus the law governing fevers has been wiped out, and Grace has taken over. The same thing is true with the healing of any form of disease or inharmony.

Whenever a person is ill, it is the result of some law of disease, and each law of disease has some remedy, at least those that are considered curable. When one of these is set aside, the whole physical law concerning that is set aside, but by what? Not one single human or material reason for the fever to come down, the cold to leave, the tuberculosis to disappear or the cancer or the polio to be healed can be found. What has happened? In defiance of all material law, a state of Grace has wiped out the cause and the effect of the disease.

Materia medica, being based on cause and effect in matter, as a rule does not take into consideration a power unknown to it. That power is the power of Grace, and that is the power that sets aside every material law, every material sense of punishment, every sense of cause and effect. When you are under divine grace, there is no cause or effect: there is only Being, constant, continuous, eternal, immortal Being.

The whole of our effort is in the direction of attaining some measure of that "mind. . . which was also in Christ Jesus,"[20] because that mind is a state of Grace. That mind annuls even the laws of weather and climate, the laws of food, the laws of germs. All of these things are set aside by a divine grace which supersedes law. The law came by Moses. Grace and truth came, and still come, through the Christ. Wherever you have witnessed a spiritual healing, you have witnessed the activity of Grace annulling the law.

In this work, you do not fight error on the level of error, that is, you do not fight a material disease with a material remedy; you do not fight a mental evil with a thought. Even though acknowledging that there appears to be physical or mental

inharmony or discord, you have to rise above the level of fighting it to the level of receiving divine grace in consciousness, and
It then wipes out both cause and effect and leaves you in a state
of spiritual being. This becomes possible when you have agreed
that you need go outside your own being for anything.

You need not go outside your own being for healing, harmony, or supply, because the whole of Grace, the wholeness of
Christhood, is your own individual being, all summed up in the
one word *I*. The state of Grace or spiritual being is embodied in
the word *I*. Isaiah who knew the nature of the Christ so well
sums it up:

> But now thus saith the Lord
> that created thee, O Jacob,
> and he that formed thee, O Israel,
> Fear not: for I have redeemed thee,
> I have called thee by thy name; thou art mine.
>
> When thou passest through the waters,
> I will be with thee; and through the rivers,
> they shall not overflow thee:
> when thou walkest through the fire,
> thou shalt nor be burned;
> neither shall the flame kindle upon thee.
>
> For I am the Lord thy God,
> the Holy One of Israel, thy Savior: . . .
>
> Since thou wast precious in my sight,
> thou hast been honourable,
> and I have loved thee:
> therefore will I give men for thee,
> and people for thy life.
>
> Fear not: for I am with thee: I will bring thy seed

> from the east, and gather thee from the west;
> I will say to the north, Give up; and to the south,
> Keep not back: bring my sons from far,
> and my daughters from the ends of the earth;
>
> Even everyone that is called by my name:
> for I have created him for my glory,
> I have formed him; yea,
> I have made him.
>
> Isaiah 43:1-7.

Have you ever stopped to realize that God formed us for His glory? You would think we made ourselves, the way we worry about ourselves. God formed us for His purpose and His plan, even everyone that is called by His name. "For I have created him for my glory, I have formed him; yea, I have made him."

TAPE RECORDED EXCERPTS
Prepared by the Editor

When the world is too much with us, it is helpful to remember that our true purpose in life is that we may be a transparency through which the glory of God can shine. Then, we become beholders of God as the activity of our life, and we have the joy of being instruments through which the inner glory shines.

Be a Transparency

"We can only be instruments through which the voice of God comes, and that makes us very humble, because we know that 'I can of mine own self do nothing.' I never will get so spiritual that I can do anything except be a transparency through which the voice of God can speak. . . . The further we go, the more of a transparency we will be because of our nothingness. We no longer speak to God; we no longer try to influence God or use God. We know enough now to be a clean window pane to let the light shine through. . . . Our new attitude of life will always be keeping the ear open."

Joel S. Goldsmith, "The Nature of God, Error, and Prayer," *The 1963 Instructions for Teaching the Infinite Way.*

Chapter Five

Contemplative Meditation and Healing Work

Yet now hear, O Jacob my servant;
and Israel, whom I have chosen:

Thus saith the Lord that made thee, and formed thee
from the womb, which will help thee; Fear not,
O Jacob, my servant; and thou,
Jesurun, whom I have chosen.

For I will pour water upon him that is thirsty,
and floods upon the dry ground:
I will pour my spirit upon thy seed, and my blessing
upon thine offspring: . . .

One shall say, I am the Lord's; and another shall
call himself by the name of Jacob; . . .

Thus saith the Lord the King of Israel,
and his redeemer the Lord of hosts;
I am the first, and I am the last;
and beside me there is no God.

Isaiah 44: 1-3, 5,6

Many believe that although we are spiritual beings we are also material, since we were materially conceived and came forth out of a physical womb. But in these verses there is evidence that even that which came from the womb is spiritually conceived: "Thus saith the Lord that made thee, and formed thee from the womb." The difference comes when we realize that we are formed by the Lord and agree that we are of the Lord.

In Isaiah, chapter 45, this principle is again repeated:

I am the Lord, and there is none else,
there is no God beside me:
I girded thee, though thou hast not known me:

That they may know from the rising of the sun,
and from the west, that there is none beside me.
I am the Lord,
and there is none else.

I form the light, and create darkness:
I make peace, . . . I the Lord do all these things.

Isaiah 45:5-7

The Miracle Word

In the very midst of us, we are carrying around the *I* that formed us, the consciousness that is responsible for our being at the point of studying a message such as this. That *I* which we carry with us will, if we but recognize Its presence, go through the flames with us so they will not kindle upon us. If we go through the waters we will not drown, for that *I* will never leave us nor forsake us.

How many *I*'s are there? There is only one. That *I* is spelled with a capital. *I* is Deity, that *I* in the midst of us is mighty, but despite that we go outside ourselves looking for God and seeking safety and security:

I in the midst of thee am mighty.
I in the midst of thee formed thee
before ever you were in the womb.

This *I,* which is our true identity, formed us. We have missed the point that we ourselves constitute the unity of Father, son, and Holy Ghost. God is the Father, God is the son, and God is the communion between the Father and the son. The fullness of that is in every person when he realizes the *I* within him.

I is the miracle word of all time. It is the word that Moses used when he discovered the truth of his own *I Amness:* "I Am That I Am."[1] *I* am that *I* in the midst of me, the same *I* that King Solomon discovered when he tried to give the world the secret that would save and emancipate all mankind. He promised that at the right time and the right place he would give the word that would make every man free of human conditions. The promise was that if a person knew the words *I Am,* he could travel in all foreign places, any place, and wherever he was he could command a master's wages, just by knowing *I Am.*

That is true today of everyone who realizes what Isaiah meant, and what Jesus later confirmed:

I will never leave thee, nor forsake thee.
Hebrews 13:5

Before Abraham was, I am.
John 8:58

I am with you alway, even unto the end of the world.
Matthew 28:20

Was he talking about Jesus Christ? No, because Jesus himself said:

If I go not away,
the Comforter will not come unto you.

John 16:7

And I will pray the Father,
and he shall give you another Comforter,
that he may abide with you forever;

Even the Spirit of truth;
whom the world cannot receive,
because it seeth him not,
neither knoweth him:
but ye know him; for he dwelleth with you,
and shall be in you.

John 14:16,17

That was the *I* he was talking about when he said, "Before Abraham was, I am" with you unto the end of the world. "I will never leave you, nor forsake you." Try it. Say, *"I, I, I."*

What the Hebrew masters were trying to say was that the Messiah would come. And It has come. "Before Abraham was," It had come, and It has come to us to remain "unto the end of the world." The Messiah, or the Christ, is *I Am. I* will never leave you, nor forsake you. *I* will be with you through the flames and through the waters.

Closer Than Breathing

As we dwell in that truth and let that truth dwell in us, gradually it becomes a part of our consciousness, until eventually it takes over our whole consciousness. Then we do not live any more: It lives Itself through us.

Everyone who has lived by inspiration, whether an artist, a musician, or an inventor, knows that there is something living his life besides his human limited selfhood. That something is the *I* within him which is the very Christ, the son of God, the

Messiah, or Emmanuel, God with us. They all mean the same thing: Omnipresence.

The Presence is always with us, and It is not a Presence that is necessarily in us. It is a Presence that *is* us. That Presence is our very being. It is not in our life: It is our life. It is not in our consciousness: It is our being. It is the very fabric of our body. That is why the body should never age; that is why the body should never deteriorate because there is an *I* at the center of our being, the great *I Am*.

"Closer is he than breathing, and nearer than hands and feet."[2] What is it that is closer to us than breathing and nearer than hands and feet, if not that *I?* The only thing that is closer than breathing and nearer than hands and feet is *I Am*. *I Am* in the midst of us is "closer than breathing, and nearer than hands and feet."

As we recognize It in the midst of us, we never let our vision go outside to anybody or anything, but we dwell at the center of our being in the recognition of this truth, and in silence, until that *I* announces Itself to us. One of these days it will announce Itself to us and will say to us, "*I* am with you."

Some years ago, groups of Infinite Way students in Hawaii used to go swimming together. We would swim out some distance and then have a lesson in truth. One day, as I was swimming out, the voice within said, "In a few days you are going to be in trouble, but have no fear because *I* will be there and although you may not be able to know it at that minute or feel it, do not fear because *I* will be there taking care of the situation." When we get a promise like that from within, we really don't care what is coming, because nothing matters as long as It is going to take over.

A few days later I took a plane from Hawaii to California, and when we were out just about one hour, the engine to the left of me began to do a little put-putting, which I recognized as not normal for engines under those conditions. I thought, "Ah hah! here it is!" But I had no fear because I knew that the promise had been given. The pilot seemed to pay no attention to it, although he probably was trying to correct it. Soon it began again, and again he did nothing about it. This time I felt a little strange, but the voice came again, "The next time he will." The third time it happened, the pilot swung us right around and back to Hawaii. It turned out that there was a choke in the feed-line, and had we gone on we would have run out of gas just two hours before arriving in San Francisco, which would have been an awkward place to run out of fuel.

Grace Frees Us From Dependence on Externals

We bring the day nearer when we live by divine grace if, first of all, we agree that there is an *I* within and can feel that it is true. Nobody can live this life without having some kind of inner assurance that it is true. The mystical literature of the world reveals that every mystic, from earliest India right up to the present, has found that the kingdom of God is within, that the one spiritual Selfhood, sometimes called the Oversoul, is right here where we are.

With that knowledge we would begin to withdraw our faith and reliance from whatever or whomever it is that we have been depending upon outside ourselves. Whether it is God, a husband, a wife, a parent, a position, or an investment, we would begin to withdraw our dependence upon those, not the use of them—the use of them is convenient—but the dependence on them, and realize:

> The good in my experience
> must flow out from me.
> The I within me goes before me
> to make the crooked places straight."[3]
> That very I which is called God,
> the son of God, the Christ,
> that spiritual presence,

that power is that which walks beside me
as protection and comes
behind me as a rear guard.

By whatever name we give It, It is divine grace. Grace in the scriptures or in Infinite Way writings means a state of consciousness that banishes, annihilates, and wipes out physical and mental law, the law of cause and effect, and enables us to live by that.

Releasing the Power of Grace

Since all this is within us, there must be a way for us to release It. At the present time in most of us this power of Grace is very much like a tightly closed rosebud. It cannot be a flower, it cannot give off its perfume, it cannot give off its beauty until it is opened. It will not do to try to pluck it open from the outside. Some spiritual law operates from within and opens it from the within to the without.

So it is with us. Let us assume for a moment that the kingdom of God is within us, but that we have seen very little evidence of it and have had very little benefit from it, so that many times we even doubt if it is true. But now we agree that it is reasonable that this kingdom of God is within us, and that here where we are the allness of God is expressed.

Let us now take the next step and agree that within us is the intelligence of God, the life of God, the love of God, the joy of God, the spirit of God, the immortality of God. All this is the splendor of God, and it is imprisoned within you and me. Robert Browning tells us that we must open out a way for "the imprisoned splendor" to escape rather "than in effecting entry for a light supposed to be without." The prayers of the world have been an attempt to get the splendor of God to come to us, but the secret of prayer is that we must open our inner Being, our inner Selfhood, our inner Christhood and make a way for the infinite nature of God's being, the splendor of God, to escape from us into the without. In doing that we bless not only ourselves but all who come within range of our consciousness. The Master tells us over and over that it is not you or I who do the work of blessing but "the imprisoned splendor" escaping out into the world of men where it can touch them and influence them.

How Meditation Opens the Door

Opening a way for the imprisoned splendor to escape is through meditation. One of the best ways to meditate, more especially in the beginning stages of meditation, is what I call contemplative meditation: the contemplation of God and of the things of God. When the contemplation, which in itself is a mental activity, stops, then must follow a listening period in which we do not think but take the attitude of listening as if we were holding our ear open expecting to hear something. It is in that period following the contemplative meditation that the whole experience takes place. The contemplation of God and the things of God is our preparation for the release, the opening out of the way, the realization, demonstration, or experience of God.

That quiet moment afterwards, when we hold ourselves in a listening attitude, is when the very spirit of God Itself breaks through and in one way or another lets us know that It is on the field, sometimes by a deep breath, sometimes by a feeling which might be thought of as a "click", sometimes as a passage of scripture or some other spiritual writing, sometimes like a weight falling off our shoulder, a sense of release as if the whole world had dropped away and we had no more troubles or problems.

It probably will never come in the same way twice, so let us never try to hold on to an experience of yesterday, yesterday's manna, or yesterday's statements of truth. Always in this contemplative state, we are alert and awake for God to announce Itself in some new, higher form, or some form suitable to the occasion of the moment. Follow me as you read a contemplative meditation I experienced, remembering that the words you read are the first part of the meditation. Let the first word of every meditation be God:

> God, God, God, God—God, the very presence
> within me, God, the only power of the universe.
> The only power? Yes, the only power.
> There is no power other than God, and God has said,
> "Beside me there is no God,"
> no other presence.
> How wonderful!

> How wonderful that there are
> no laws of disease, no laws of death!
> There is only spiritual law, God the lawgiver,
> God the Law, and all of this closer to me
> than breathing, within my very own being.
> I do not have to reach out anywhere to God.

> And God is the all-knowing
> intelligence of this universe.
> God it is that created this universe
> and formed it. God it is that created me
> and formed me, God, the all-knowing wisdom.
> Then can I tell God of my need?
> No, God is the all-knowing
> wisdom and intelligence.

> God is love.
> Then need I remind God that I need food,
> clothing, health, housing?
> No, I take no thought for my life.
> God is the intelligence of this universe

that formed me in the beginning
and must know my need
even before I ask.
Furthermore, God is divine love,
and it is God's good pleasure
to give me the kingdom.
Then I must not go to God
to ask for anything.
I must accept God's grace as my sufficiency.

God in the midst of me is mighty,
and it is God's good pleasure that
I bear fruit richly, God's good pleasure.
God created me for His glory.
I do not have to tell God what I need
or for whom it is needed.
I do not have to tell God
to remove a fever or a lump.
The all-knowing intelligence within me
knows my need, and it is Its good pleasure
to give it to me. God is love.
God is life eternal.
God is the very soul and spirit of my being.

I have been told to lean not
unto my own understanding,
but to acknowledge Him in all my ways.
I acknowledge God as the intelligence
of my being, the intelligence which knows
enough to maintain my mind and soul
and body in health and harmony and purity.
I acknowledge God to be my hidden talents.
I acknowledge God to be my hidden strength.
I acknowledge God in all my ways.

I know that of mine own self I am nothing,
of my own self I can do nothing,
but I know that God, the Father within me,
can do all things.
"He performeth the thing that is appointed for me."[4]
This very He in the center of my being
performs every task that is given me to do.
I have the strength and the understanding through
Grace to perform everything I am called upon to do.

"Greater is he that is in you, than he that is
the world."[5] He that is within me,
the Father within me, is greater than any problem.
Why? Because no problem in and of itself has power.
God, the great power, the all-power,
the only power, right here where I am!
"Son, thou art ever with me,
and all that I have is thine.[6] . . .
He performeth the thing that is appointed for me.[4] . . .
He maketh me lie down in green pastures:
he leadeth me beside the still waters. . . .
Yea, though I walk through the valley
of the shadow of death," [7]
He walks right there with me, for He and I are one.

That He will never leave me is a divine spiritual
promise which has come down to us from the ages,
even before there was a Hebrew testament.
I, I will never leave me.
I, the great God, the only God, the one power,
the one presence, the allness of good
will never leave me nor forsake me.
Whither should I flee, whither could I flee
from the spirit of God?

God neither gives nor withholds, but always eternally
is, divinely is, ever present, all power, all wisdom.
So I have no desires except to know God aright.

The contemplative meditation can follow along that line or
can come as something entirely original with you. The main
thing is that you leave your problem and your self outside, and
become only a contemplative, a beholder, a witness. Let your
whole contemplation be of God—the nature of God, the nature
of God's laws, the nature of God's grace, the nature of God's
life—until you arrive at that place where you have an inner feeling of being able to rest and listen for the Father.

Meditation Becomes a Necessity

Eventually meditation becomes a way of life. First you
meditate once or twice a day according to your own drive. But
if you ever get to the point of meditating three times a day,
you are lost: God's got you and you are "hooked but good"!
This is because after you have experienced meditation within
yourself three times a day, you will have to meditate four times
and after you get to six, you will find that at three o'clock in
the morning you awaken. You cannot sleep after three o'clock
without meditating because you cannot wait until morning to
meditate again.

You cannot get along any more without the realization of
God than you can do without your best beloved. You discover
that you have never loved anyone on earth as you love that
presence and power. That is why it is sometimes possible to
leave mother and father, sister and brother, husband and wife
"for my sake," because the intensity of that love and devotion
grows with the experience to a place where it becomes prayer
"without ceasing."[8]

Even after you have had the experience of meditation in the
morning, you cannot sit down at the breakfast table without

saying, "Thank You, Father." Half a dozen times before noon something will take place in your experience and you will be saying, "Thank You, Father." Something will continuously be operating within you to keep the word God, Father, or Love present where you are.

It is through this growing remembrance of God that a point of transition takes place. This contemplation of God and the things of God becomes so constant, even while you are working, about your business, driving a car, or doing housework that one day a point of transition comes. After that you do not meditate any more. It does it continuously through you. It keeps voicing Itself in you. It keeps saying, "Don't worry, I am right here sitting on your shoulder." There is not an hour of the day when in some way or other It is not voicing Itself to you, making a smile come to your face.

Healing Through Clear Vision

I have said that someday all healing work will be done with a smile. Why? Suppose that as you looked at some beautiful flowers your vision was not clear and you saw them as of dark and black colors that ran into each other, so that both the color and the form were indistinct. Then someone put glasses on you, and you said, "Oh, so that's the way it is." From then on, using your glasses, the flowers are always beautiful. If someone were to come along and say, "Isn't it too bad how those flowers are blurred and darkened," you would respond, "Oh, no, they are perfect and bright." He would of course be surprised at your saying this.

That is what happens in healing work. Somebody with blurred spiritual vision says, "I am sick; I am poor; I am dying; I am old; I am unemployed." The person who has attained the fourth-dimensional consciousness, Christ-consciousness, responds with, "I do not see any of that. It isn't there." And it really isn't! God is too pure to behold iniquity. It is only to the unillumined human consciousness that there is any blur of discord or sin on the face of the globe, no iniquity, no sin, disease, or death. If there were, some way would have to be found to remove it, some way other than God, because if there is any evil on earth, God has been very lax all these thousands of years in permitting it to be here.

There is no use turning to God to remove sin, disease, or death, but you cannot know that through the three-dimensional mind because it is judging by the evidence of your distorted vision, blurring the scene. It is only as your spiritual sight is opened that you are able to look right at the person, place, or thing where the sin or the disease appears and say, "Neither do I condemn thee: go, and sin no more.".... Today shalt thou be with me in paradise."[10] Why? You are not aware of any evil.

Gautama's Great Revelation

The spiritually illumined are not aware of evil as a reality, although they are conscious of it as a claim, an appearance, a suggestion, or temptation in human thought. The truly spiritually illumined know that this world is full of the appearance of sin, disease, and death. But they know that their spiritual illumination wipes it out, because they see through the appearance to the reality.

Gautama was shocked and horrified when he saw sin, disease, death, and poverty on earth. In the way he had been reared, he had never been permitted to witness these things. As he went out in the world and became aware that such things do exist on earth, he set out to find the secret of a life without sin, disease, or death. He knew that those things were wrong, that they had no right to be. He was horrified and left all his riches and splendor to go out into the world searching out all the masters who were known in India, but no one could give him the answer. Some told him that if he fasted he would find the answer, and others told him other things.

For twenty-one years he tried every method that was known, including virtual starvation in order to become spiritual. He became an ascetic. Then one day when he was bathing in the sacred river Ganges, he was so weak from lack of food that he could not pull himself out. He nearly drowned. When he did get out he realized that what he had been doing could not be right, knowing that he was so weak that if God had appeared he would not have been able to recognize It. After that, he went out, ate, and took care of himself until he brought his body back to normal. But in so doing he lost all his disciples. They said, "This man is not spiritual. This man is eating food; this man is resting; this man is not an ascetic. Why, we have been wrong about him." And they all left him.

When he was alone and his body was again functioning normally, he sat down under the bodhi tree and meditated all night long. Then came the revelation to him: all sin, disease, and death are illusion. They have no existence. With that realization he had attained the Fourth Dimensional consciousness or Christ-consciousness, which knows that all these negative appearances have no existence outside the mind which is accepting these false suggestions.

Seeing Through Appearances

To a man in delirium tremens, the snakes or pink elephants he sees are real, but to you they are not real, and because they are not real, you do not struggle against the snakes or the elephants. You sit patiently and quietly until through your quietness the man struggling with such a suggestion becomes quiet. Then when he opens his eyes he says, "Thank you. You have taken away my snakes and pink elephants." He see you as having great power, being a great healer. But you did not take away his snakes or his elephants, because there were none: there was a distorted vision, a disturbed vision. Peace was restored to him because you waited in confidence.

As you sit in quietness beside a sick, a sinning, or a dying person, without thinking without declaring any truth, without trying to remove snakes, elephants, cancers, or tumors, just by sitting in that quietness and confidence until the peace of God descends upon you, the patient opens his eyes and says, "I'm healed."

In the first year of my practice, a man was brought to me who had tuberculosis and who had been given up and sent home from a sanitarium to die with his family. He decided to try our work before giving up all hope, so he was brought to my office. We sat talking awhile and finally he asked me to take up work for him. As an afterthought, he added, "Can I tell you this? I have pyorrhea, and it is so bad that all my teeth are loose, and I can't brush them any more. So would you take that up at the same time?"

I agreed to do this, and we kept on talking. Then came the time for the treatment, and I was so involved with healing this dreaded tuberculosis that I forgot all about the pyorrhea. The next morning he telephoned me and asked, "What have you done to me? Why, I have been brushing my teeth for five minutes, and they are solid as can be."

"Well," I said, "you have a fine practitioner, so you don't have to worry about the tuberculosis now."

It is through just such experiences as this that you learn these great lessons of humility which teach you that you are not a good practitioner, you are not a good healer, you do not have spiritual healing power. The only spiritual power you or anyone else has is the power of recognizing the allness of Spirit. That is all. It is not a healing power. Why should God give you a healing power and not someone else? Why should there be a healing power?

As a matter of fact, how could God heal a disease if He permitted one to begin with? No, if disease existed, it would have to exist with God's grace and God's permission, and then neither you nor I, nor anyone else, could remove it. But disease in and of itself has no more reality than snakes and pink elephants in delirium tremens, not a bit. It may appear real to you, to your patient, or to your student. It may sometimes appear so real to you that you may have to ask someone else for a little help in coming to the realization of your true identity.

The Master had to ask his disciples for help. "Could ye not watch with me one hour?"[11] In other words, what he was asking was, "Couldn't you stay awake with me, give me a treatment, help me out of this mess that I'm in?" No, they couldn't; they fell asleep. So Jesus had to make the demonstration all alone. But that does not have to be. There is no reason why there should not be many who are willing to stay awake, not only for an hour, but all night long if it is necessary to establish that sense of peace.

Quietness and Confidence Open the Way for the Spirit to Take Over

The healing power is the quietness and confidence that you are able to attain when called upon for help, or that you can attain and maintain in your whole experience. Only those who have really separated themselves from the business world or from their family duties can perhaps live in it so continuously that they can be called upon any time in the twenty-four hours of the day or night and get an immediate response without having to go off somewhere and establish themselves in the quietness and calm.

Otherwise, if you are responsible for somebody's well being, if you have a family of children, parents, or someone else who is looking to you for help, the best way that you can give it to them is, first of all, to train yourself in the contemplative form of prayer or meditation, so that through contemplating God you can bring yourself to a point of quietness. Then settle into that quietness and confidence until you are overshadowed by the Holy Ghost.

Mary was overshadowed by the Holy Ghost, and then the Christ was conceived in her. That is what happens to you as you rest in quietness and confidence, in stillness. As you attain that quietness, the Holy Ghost, the Christ, is conceived in you, and then it is That which takes over your child, your relative, yourself, your affairs, and establishes harmony and peace.

Many Meditations May Be Necessary to Bring About the Requisite Adjustment

The healing work in and of itself is not difficult. There are no intricate or deep truths to be known. You have to know God, the nature of God, and the nature of prayer. You have to know that there is no use going to God for something, because God is not giving and God is not withholding. God is just *is-ing.* God is just being, always shining. What you have to do is to settle into the rhythm of God's grace, and let the Holy Ghost overshadow you until you feel that stillness, quietness, and peace. Then you can trust your patient to that stillness.

It may be necessary for one reason or another to repeat the meditation later in the day or the next day. In some cases you may have to repeat it for a whole year to bring out the healing that is necessary, for the simple reason that it is not possible to heal everyone instantaneously, no matter who you are or what you are. There are things in the consciousness of a person requiring adjustment, and the treatment or meditation you give, the peace and quiet you attain begins the very first time to bring about that adjustment. But it may take ten, thirty, sixty, ninety, or one thousand of those meditations before all the adjustments necessary to reveal the harmony that was always there at the center of being takes place.

You can begin to do healing work in any moment by realizing that if there is anyone in your life looking to you, counting on you, or depending upon you for any help, consolation, comforting, or healing, your work is to sit quietly and forget the person. You can remember him until you sit down and begin the meditation. Then you turn from the person and do not permit him to come back into your consciousness. You keep your mind stayed on God as in the foregoing contemplative meditation. Keep it thus stayed until you feel enough assurance to stop the contemplation, become quiet and at peace. Sit in that peace until you feel some kind of release, but then above all things, do not go out looking for results. Instead go to bed and go to sleep. Never look for results. Let the results show themselves forth to you. All you are responsible for is to reach that rhythm of peace, assurance, calmness, and omnipresence and then let it do the work.

Chapter Six

Spiritual Fulfillment Through Consciousness

We can bring forth in demonstration only what we have attained in consciousness. A musician or an artist can give forth no greater degree of music or art than his acquired or attained musical or artistic consciousness. A pianist, even with a highly developed technique but without a musical consciousness, cannot ever give the performance of a Paderewski, nor can an amateur artist or painter produce the work of a master. We can express only the state of consciousness which we have attained.

No life experience can ever be greater than the attained consciousness of the individual. There are thousands of attorneys in the United States, but only a few first ranking ones, because only those few have put into their work what they are now drawing out. In every walk of life a person brings forth what he has attained in consciousness.

So, too, what we attain in this work is the direct result of what we have put into the work. If we have put in time, study, meditation, and pondering, we will attain a higher consciousness than those who casually read, rarely meditate, and hardly ever study.

Do Not Try to Demonstrate Forms of Good: Demonstrate the Substance

By the grace of God, one of the most profound truths has been revealed to me, not that I am the first one to whom it was revealed. That truth can best be explained with this illustration. If I did not have a glass tumbler and wanted to make one, I would realize that there could be no tumbler without first having the glass out of which to form it. Knowing that, I am no longer concerned with having a tumbler: I am concerned now with obtaining the materials with which to make glass, because once I have the material for glass, I can make a tumbler. Actually the tumbler was not my real need: glass was my need, for in having the glass I can have the tumbler.

Let us suppose I need a table. How am I going to get one? Demonstrate it? Out of what? For a table wood is required. So let us forget the table and go out and demonstrate some wood, and then when we have the wood we can make our table, chair, or cabinet.

We think we need health, supply, safety, security, companionship, or a home. In a sense we may need those things just as we need a tumbler or a table. But this I can tell you: there is no way to demonstrate those things unless we have the substance of them. And what is their substance? The substance of health is God; the substance of supply is God; the substance of home is God; the substance of companionship is God; the substance of life eternal is God; the substance of peace, of joy, and of eternality is God, Consciousness.

Get God

We might as well give up all thought of demonstrating health, harmony, wholeness, completeness, perfection, wealth, success, or joy until we have first demonstrated the substance of which these are formed, and that substance is God. Once we have demonstrated God, we will not have to demonstrate the other things, because God constitutes the others. Do you remember, "I shall yet praise him, who is the health of my countenance, and my God"¹? There is no use seeking the health of our countenance without first seeking God. But in finding God, we will have found the health of our countenance.

God is our abiding place. Until we have found God, what is the use of seeking an abiding place? When we have found God, we will have found our abiding place. "The Lord is my rock, and my fortress; and my deliverer."² Then why go out to get a bombproof shelter? If we get God we have our fortress, and it is a fortress that not even an atomic bomb can reach.

In the Infinite Way we lose all desire to demonstrate form. That does not mean that we sit on cloud nine and say, "I don't need a tumbler; I don't need a table; I don't need health; or I don't need wealth." We do not do that, because in the human world we know we need them. But we have attained the wisdom that knows that we cannot have them unless we first have God. If we have God, we will have infinite abundance, all that is necessary, and with twelve basketsful left over.

The Infinite Way is not a message: it is an experience. It is the experience of God, and from the moment we touch the Infinite Way our entire goal becomes the attainment of the experience of God. Once we have the experience of God everything else is added to us, really not so much added to us as included in us. Having attained that realization we never will have to demonstrate anything in life. The demonstration of the form is the added thing, the included thing, that which is in and of God.

A person may want a home, furniture, an automobile, or a boat. Then someone says, "Well, why not go out and earn fifty thousand dollars and then you can buy all those things?" It is not possible spiritually to attain health, unless a realization of God has first been attained. Yes, we can attain physical health through other means, such as medication or surgery, but even after we have acquired health we may still find ourselves lonely, inadequate, unhappy, or dissatisfied. Then we may think the solution lies in accumulating greater wealth. There are many legal human ways of obtaining wealth, but having attained it, our digestion may be such that we cannot eat the food we can afford to buy. In attaining wealth, we do not necessarily attain peace of mind, peace of soul, or harmony of any kind.

In attaining a realization of God, however, we attain health, wealth, and abundance, and with it we attain harmony, contentment, and a sense of satisfaction in living.

What Is the Reason for Living?

How many people in the world actually have a good reason for living? How many people on earth really have any good reason for staying around another ten, twenty, or thirty years? For what purpose are they here? At one time a religious leader said to me that he had heard I had been called to a very elderly woman who was dying and had brought healing to her. He wanted to know why I had done it. "What is she going to do with the life that you saved for her? Knit some more booties for her grandchildren?" Probably from that standpoint he could have been right. What difference would it make whether she was on earth eating three meals a day and sleeping a few hours at night, or going on to whatever the next experience is? I have no answer to that.

The reason that I am always willing to help, and to me it is of no concern whether the person is nine years of age or ninety, or one hundred nine, is because if he received the help it is just one more evidence that a realization of God restores harmony. It can restore harmony if a person is one hundred fifty years of age. That does not necessarily mean that a physical healing will change a person's life, because if a grandmother wants to go on knitting booties for grandchildren to the exclusion of any other activity, she can go ahead, but it is not a very good reason for living.

As we look around, we cannot help but wonder sometimes why it is so important for most people to continue living. What are they doing for themselves or for the world? Eating, sleeping, half starving, illiterate, uneducated? What joy is there in life for them? Traveling the world as I have, one comes to the conclusion that there is not too much reason for three-fourths of the people of the world to go on living. They are not doing anything with their lives, not accomplishing a thing, not adding to their own well-being or to that of the world. That is the cause of their discontent and unhappiness, because everyone, whether he knows it or not, has a destiny, a spiritual destiny which few are fulfilling.

Each one of us actually represents God revealing Itself on earth. To fulfill that purpose, every day we should be accomplishing something, not only for our own improvement, but for the advancement of the world itself. When we are not doing that, we are not fulfilling ourselves, and it is no wonder that we are unhappy.

Finding Fulfillment

If a master musician were to find himself in a position where he could do nothing but play a few shows for the movies, he would be so bored and unhappy that life would no longer have any meaning for him. Nobody with the gift of real musicianship could ever be satisfied just to sit and drum out a little boogie-woogie.

When we feel within ourselves a call to something higher and then find ourselves doing nothing or next to nothing, we become dissatisfied and discontented. That very discontent has been the cause of much evil in the world because it has made some persons too ambitious for the development and fulfillment of their ego instead of their God-capacities. It is persons of that type who become the dictators of the world throughout the ages and in every generation. Inwardly such persons feel the call to be something more than an army corporal, something more than a nonentity, but not knowing how to fulfill that need in accordance with God's plan, they go ahead according to their own ego, and fight their way to high places.

The latter part of the nineteenth century in the United States was the era of the robber barons, men who acquired fortunes of one hundred to two hundred million dollars by plundering railroads, steamship companies, or bankrupting one company after another to increase their personal wealth. Actually what prompted these people was their inner urge for expression, for accomplishment, for achievement, something every one of us at sometime or other has felt. But instead of letting it evolve through God's plan, they fed their own egos.

Just the opposite of that is exemplified in a man who early recognized that he was a genius, a great inventor and a great engineer. He formed a manufacturing company and became successful in a very short time. Then with little warning the company collapsed, and he went bankrupt. He could not understand how that could happen, because he knew that he was a better manufacturer of his particular product than anybody in the business. Nevertheless, he went bankrupt.

While he was going through the process of bankruptcy, he spent hours and hours at a time in daily introspection, trying to find out why this had happened and what had brought it upon him. Then one day the realization came, "I know; I left God out of my business. That is the whole thing, but I will never let that happen again. God is going to become a partner in my new business, and I'm going to credit Him with ten percent of the profits."

This he did. He began tithing, not merely by making out a check, but he saw to it that money went into places where it would accomplish some good according to his light of good, and then such success began to come that in a few years he was giving eighty percent of his income to God in the form of contributions to worthwhile causes. Yet, in so doing he still had four million dollars each year left over.

The moment we admit God into our experience as a partner, acknowledge God as the source of whatever good there is in our lives, acknowledge God as intelligence, wisdom, direction, knowledge, whatever it may be that we claim of good, our energies not only cannot be misdirected, but we are directed to some type of fulfilling activity that gives us a good reason for living and for being on earth.

At one time I was very close to death, so close that I knew it was only a matter of a few hours before I might go on. In that experience the realization came to me that it would be futile for me to die, that I had never done anything on earth that would even repay my mother for her birth pains. How foolish it would be to leave this earth without accomplishing something worthwhile, at least as a way of saying, "Thank you," to her for her part in bringing me into the world. That was the turning point, and I awakened in the morning healed.

The realization that my life up to that time had been nothing but a human experience, that it had accomplished nothing more than to earn a living, give a little of it away, but really to do nothing of a worthwhile or creative nature, gave me back my health and led ultimately to all the activity that has followed. Now I have no hesitation or concern should the call to leave this plane come at any moment. Some people have been benefitted because I passed this way.

If there is an unhappy person, it is because he is not fulfilling himself, nor has he found that which gives him any lasting satisfaction. There are some persons who are being fulfilled in being mothers, and that is certainly worthwhile, but all persons cannot be fulfilled in that way, not even all women. Some men are fulfilled in being successful, successful in whatever their work may be, but all men cannot be satisfied with that. Each one must find what fulfills him in order to have a full and complete life. If he finds it through realization of God, he will have found contentment, peace, joy, and with it come health and wholeness.

Communion

When the realization of God comes, there is a flow between God and us. That is communion. It bears little relationship to the orthodox concept of communion. Communion is not an external experience. Communion is something that takes place within ourselves. It is an inner experience with God, the Christ, or our inner Self. In that communion the spirit of God, which is the grace of God, the power of God, the presence of God, flows in and through our whole being—our mind and soul and body,—and in that experience we attain God's grace, God's peace, God's supply, God's allness. A communion that does not attain that flow inside is not real communion. It is only an effort in the right direction.

Communion is complete when we have the feeling of an answer within us, of having made contact with our source. A warmth, a glow, a sense of release, or a smile that comes spontaneously, descends upon us. We cannot account for it because of any external reason. It is just there because we are at-one; we are in communion. The result of that communion is the descent of the Holy Ghost, a sense of being enfolded in the spirit of God. That, of course, is the object of all our study and meditation.

Sometimes we use the word *communion* in place of prayer or treatment. In the early days on the path we may use the word *treatment,* and as we go on we may think of ourselves as being in prayer. The day comes, however, when prayer takes on such a different meaning that we drop that, too. We do not treat any more and we do not pray any more in the commonly accepted sense of prayer, but we understand that the secret of life is communion.

Adequate Preparation Makes
for a Deeper Spiritual Experience

When we are in communion with God, the flow of God is going on through us, and that results in a sense of peace, joy, power, a flowing out to all those who are in touch with us. That is the meaning of the statement, "And I, if I be lifted up from the earth, will draw all men unto me."[3] If I am in communion, if I am in conscious contact with God so that the flow of God permeates me, then those who are receptive must inevitably receive some measure of lifting up through that.

The degree of enlightenment received varies with the individual in terms of the preparation he has put into attaining God-realization. In trying to be as good a human being as possible, in loving our neighbor as ourselves, meditating, studying, and trying to contact the Christ within, we are on the path that leads to Christ-realization. If the meditations are carried on and deepen, those meditations will lead to the spiritual experience of Christ-consciousness.

If it is possible to meditate with a person who had gone a step beyond us, that is, one who has attained the ability or the capacity for being an instrument for spiritual healing or teaching, that makes for greater preparation and quickens the process. The degree of the illumination of the spiritual teacher facilitates the degree to which we are drawn up in meditation to illumination. That is the way of the schools of wisdom in which those who have become teachers, or masters, that is, those who have attained illumination, lift the students up into that experience.

If a person comes to the spiritual path as a human being out of a human world with no preparation, he is not likely to have the experience at all. If a person has come with some preparation, he may feel a little of that gentle presence. If he has come with deep preparation, it may be a very deep experience.

It is individual consciousness that determines the depth of the experience. If Jesus Christ had been talking to us, perhaps half of those to whom he spoke would go out the next day and help crucify him, while the other half would have been lifted right into heaven.

Communion enriches our spiritual development and transforms us from the educated, reasoning mind to that "mind. . .

which was also in Christ Jesus."[4] That mind never has to analyze, never has to reason, and always is given the answer to whatever is presented to it.

The Difference Between
Cosmic and Spiritual Consciousness

We have been living primarily through the human mind, which in and of itself is an activity of awareness and not a power. Therefore, we have never been able to accomplish with the mind the things we thought we wanted to accomplish because the mind is not a creative faculty. Behind the mind, however, there are what might be called two different degrees of awareness: one, the cosmic mind or cosmic consciousness, and the other spiritual consciousness.

Through the human mind-level we know, perceive, and learn. Through it we attain knowledge and are able to make use of our talents. But behind the human mind is the cosmic mind or cosmic consciousness, the source from which we draw the things of this world: art, literature, science, invention, or discovery. These all come through from cosmic consciousness, and because cosmic consciousness is the great storehouse of the laws of this earth, our great inventors have gone beyond the human mind to cosmic consciousness to draw forth such inventions as the automobile, airplane and television. Much of our art and some of our music, too, have come from the cosmic because those at that stage of consciousness are attuned to the world of art, science, literature, invention, and discovery. Although cosmic consciousness is not Christ-consciousness, it is the same form of activity as Christ-consciousness except that it is on the human level.

One can be attuned to cosmic consciousness and yet not attuned to spiritual consciousness, because cosmic consciousness and spiritual consciousness are not the same. A person may have cosmic consciousness and yet have not a trace of spirituality. In the same way it is possible to be attuned to Christ-consciousness and not draw forth from the cosmic.

We have little evidence of the spiritual masters having had much access to the cosmic realm. When we use the term *cosmic consciousness,* it should be understood that it refers to the consciousness of human wisdom. Spiritual consciousness refers to the realm of spiritual wisdom.

When Thomas A. Edison, who was very close to God, but was considered an atheist because he did not believe in going to church, was at work in his laboratories, his method of work was to become very still, hold his ear out, and then he would be able to direct his engineers to the next step they were to take. There are persons who can immediately give the answers to complicated mathematical computations without a process of any kind. That is cosmic consciousness at work. There is no need for thinking, reasoning, or figuring: it is a knowing without a process.

There is yet a deeper level of awareness and that is spiritual consciousness, known or called by such different names as the fourth-dimensional consciousness, Christ-consciousness, or the Buddha-mind. It is to this source that we turn for spiritual wisdom and for the grace and love of God. Of course, it is not that we decide that today we are going to bringing forth music, so we turn to the cosmic mind or that today we are seeking spiritual wisdom, so we turn off the cosmic and turn on spiritual consciousness. It is not like that at all. It is only that those who are attuned to the level of bringing forth the laws which govern this earth are attuned to the cosmic level and there is nothing to prevent their also being attuned to spiritual consciousness. Few of them are, however, as we can know from the manner of their human lives. Many persons have had great talents on the cosmic level and have had no awareness of spiritual consciousness.

Those engaged in spiritual activity usually think primarily of going within to become aware of spiritual consciousness. Sometimes in doing so they touch the cosmic and bring forth a greater human experience than they have known before, even finding new directions in their lives.

Spiritual Companionship

Although the object of our work is not primarily to produce health out of sickness or wealth out of lack, those are the added things. Those who catch even a grain of spiritual perception are showing forth better health and living more prosperous, happier, and more useful lives. But this is not the goal. The goal is the attaining of spiritual consciousness, so that we can behold God's creation, God's universe, so that we can commune with God and with one another, not just with each other humanly.

Our most joyous outer human companionship becomes more worthwhile if we have attained some measure of spiritual companionship. That, we can have, not because we are studying the same books, because we belong to the same church, or because we live under the same flag. The one thing that does ensure harmonious companionship is to be united in a spiritual bond due to our having attained some measure of spiritual light or consciousness. Then we can find companionship with those of any nation or of any political or religious conviction, because there will be no barrier once we have perceived the nature of their being as it really is. That being has no nationality, no race, no religion. The reality of a person's being is God, the Christ. Once we can discern that through inner spiritual vision, we do have a relationship that is eternal on earth and forever afterwards.

Spiritual Consciousness, the Goal

When we go back deep into consciousness, our mind receives truth from within, from the storehouse which is Christ-consciousness, God-consciousness, or spiritual consciousness. Up from that infinite storehouse come these truths as the voice of God uttering Itself and making the whole world of appearances melt. In that awareness, all of the apparently terrifying powers of the world shrivel, disappear, and are no more.

We are told that not even the smell of smoke is left. But in order to demonstrate so clearly that there is not even the smell of smoke we must demonstrate spiritually. It is no good to put out a fire. The smell of smoke will be left. With spiritual vision, however, we behold that there is no fire; there is no power but God, and the only fire there is, is the fire of God's love. When we try to demonstrate from the standpoint of good health replacing ill health, we are likely to have visible scars left. When we demonstrate spiritual consciousness, there are no yesterdays to remember; there are no ill effects from yesterday; there is no convalescing from yesterday. There is only the eternal now.

The development of spiritual consciousness is really the greatest attainment there is for us because in the degree of this attained consciousness, we are enabled to see spiritual form, spiritual life, spiritual beauty, and the spiritual harmony of God's creating. It is not the development of the mind; it is not thinking that we know more than we knew before: it is a matter of attaining a depth of inner awareness that expresses itself, not so much in words as in a feeling.

As Christ-consciousness or spiritual consciousness comes through, It transforms the physical appearance into the spiritual reality, which with our three dimensional eyes we see merely as an improved body or an improved pocketbook, but that is not what is actually there. Only spiritual consciousness which is the fruitage of communion reveals that.

Spiritual Consciousness Needs No Human Reliance

There are persons who are in contact with human beings from the other side and receive guidance in their business or personal affairs. The value of that would be just about the same as if we had someone in whom we had confidence on this plane to give us guidance in our affairs, but beyond that it has no demonstrated value at this time in spiritual living, and it may detract from our spiritual progress. Spiritualism, or communicating with those who have gone on, is a human activity. Whether or not it has any place in human affairs, I do not know. It has nothing to do with spiritual living; it has nothing to do with God: it merely has to do with whether or not we can communicate with one another here and continue to communicate after one of us has left this physical plane. It is still a conversation, a discussion, or a teaching with or by human beings. There is nothing spiritual about it.

Sooner or later, we who are on the spiritual path must learn that "I and my Father are one,"⁵ and that the Father within is the great *I Am*. Then when we need or require anything, we must learn to turn to that withinness, and not depend on some person, some thing, or some condition, either on this plane or another. Eddie Rickenbacker, in a rubber life boat, lost in the midst of the Pacific, with no hope of food or water, could sit with folded arms and for three weeks be fed, and not only he but the six men who were with him. That sounds impossible, but it actually happened.

For three weeks that man waited while birds came down, sat on his head, and provided food for the men to eat. Fish jumped out of the sea into the boat. The men had no fishing lines; they had no guns, no human means of being fed, but for three weeks they were fed every day, and not only that but water, fresh rainwater, fell out of a cloudless sky, so that they were even provided with water for three weeks and then ultimately rescued. If we were depending on the advice of our banker or our broker or if we were depending on our parents, or depending on somebody who had passed on, of what avail would that be if we were sitting out there in the Pacific?

The experience of Eddie Rickenbacker may be an extreme case, and although we probably never will be placed in such a predicament, every day some of us are in the position of having a need, of requiring fulfillment of one nature or another. We turn usually to human sources and resources for that fulfillment, until one day we find that even though we may be fulfilled on the physical plane, there still is an inner lack. Then it is that we learn what we have learned in Infinite Way work that there is no satisfaction unless we have the conviction that God is, that God is available, God is at hand, God is omnipresent, God is fulfillment, God is divine grace.

Until we come to that realization, we have not fulfilled ourselves in life. We have not completed our mission on earth, and we return over and over and over again to this human experience until the day does come when we can realize that God *is* and that He governs our life.

TAPE RECORDED EXCERPTS
Prepared by the Editor

In Matthew, Jesus, the harbinger of peace, promised not peace but a sword. What is this "sword"? What is the sword of the Spirit and what is its function? The excerpts from the recordings given below throw much enlightenment on this greatly misunderstood term:

The Sword of the Spirit

"Principles should be taken into our consciousness and practiced until we become so skilled in living them that they become a very part of our being and begin to live us. It is only in the beginning of any study that there is labor involved, and it makes no difference whether you are studying to be an automobile mechanic or studying to be a spiritual seer. There is hard labor involved, hard work. The sword of the Spirit must be used to cut away our old beliefs, to cut away our material foundations, our mental foundations, so that we may be established in our spiritual armor. These principles won't do it for us. It is the *practice*, the imbibing of the principles, the making them a part of our very consciousness that transmutes our lives, transforms our lives. . . .

"It seems difficult at first to stop struggling for effects, but that is where the sword of the Spirit comes in. The sword of the Spirit compels each one of us ultimately to give up the search and struggle for effect, and turn our search and struggle for Cause. . . . A spiritual teaching reverses the entire material picture. It tells us that we do not live by bread but by the Word, and not your word or mine, but by the word of God, the spirit of God in us. It tells us that the effects that we witness in life are given to us by this omnipotence or omnipresence, and that it is through living in omnipotence and omnipresence and omniscience that the effects appear as they are needed. Spiritual living stops our struggling for effects. It keeps us from trying to demonstrate our daily bread. It compels us to relax in a realization of our true identity as children of God. . . .

"The peace of the Master, the gentleness of the Master, and the comfort of the Master come only after the sword of the Spirit has separated us from our physical and mental powers, when the sword of the Spirit has cut us off from human resources and made us completely dependent on the inner Infinite Invisible. There is within us an infinite storehouse, and that infinite storehouse of life is available to you and to me. . . .

"As we listen to this, it is very sweet, very, very sweet, and seems gentle, but as we chew our cud and think it over, we find that it has particles of dynamite in it; and that dynamite is the sword of the Spirit. It is that sword of the Spirit that disturbs us because it cuts us off from dependence on things and thoughts. . . . When you are faced with life, don't trust any thoughts that are in print. Turn to God for His thoughts, and you will find that when you receive God's word in your consciousness it is literally true, 'He uttered his voice, the earth melted.' When God utters Its word in you, the earth of error—sin, disease, death, lack, and limitation—melts away."

Joel S. Goldsmith, "Summary of the Class on the Infinite Way," *The Second 1956 Steinway Hall Practitioners' Class.*

"The sword of the Spirit must come to us to sever all of our beliefs in some far-off God, sever all of our theological beliefs about. . . a God who punishes or a God who rewards, a God who gives or a God who withholds. All of this must be taken from us. . . . We will meet God face to face only when we hear the 'still small voice' within us say that little word I:

I am here. I am deathless.
Neither life nor death can separate me
from the love of God,
for I am deathless;
I am immortal; I am eternal.
I am God's own Selfhood
expressed in an infinite individual way,
but I must live, not by human wisdom,
not by my physical strength,
not by my education or my bank account. . .
I must learn to live by every word
that proceedeth out of the mouth of God.

Until this has been accomplished, the sword will continue to cut and cut and cut until it has cut away from us everything not necessary to the life of the son of God. . . .

"If we could think of ourselves as living today, and not only seeking the realization of God's grace, but realizing that there is a sufficiency of God's grace with which to meet today, each day then would take care of itself until yesterday and today and tomorrow would all melt into each other."

Joel S. Goldsmith, "The Sword of the Spirit,"
The 1963 London Work.

Chapter Seven

The Cornerstone of Spiritual Healing and Living

To be an instrument for healing work, it is necessary to know the nature of God and the nature of the son of God. Then we will never try to make a sick person well, try to stop a pain, or try to save a dying person. Our whole attitude will be, "Thank God, my spiritual vision enables me to see the son of God." The ability to realize that God constitutes individual being, and because of that, individual being is intact, is what constitutes pure spiritual healing.

The Difference Between Mental and Spiritual Healing

Literally speaking, practitioners are not healers, nor do they have any healing ability. They are persons who have received the understanding that God constitutes individual being, and therefore, individual being is spiritual and intact. That has nothing to do with changing a person, his body, or his health. It has to do with realizing that individual being is intact because of its God-nature. To that understanding must be added meditation and communion until the realization comes. That is what constitutes a practitioner.

A practitioner never has good healing ability or God-power to heal, because there is no such thing in God's kingdom. If God had any need of healing, He would do it Himself. There is no healing to be done. God's universe is intact. A practitioner is a person who knows that truth and never tries to change it.

Mental healing rests on an entirely different basis from spiritual healing. It is concerned with a mental cause for a physical effect. If the mental cause is found, presumably the physical effect is removed. But it does not always happen that way.

In spiritual healing, there is no healing process. A marital problem is approached in the same way as a physical, mental, moral, or financial one. We approach every problem with the spiritual realization that God constitutes individual being. God is the life of individual being, the soul, the spirit, the mind; and the body is the temple of the living God. That all has to do with the word *is:* is, not will be.

God as Individual Being

I have forever been grateful to the man who was my Christian Science teacher because in one of his Association addresses, when he was asked how to protect a treatment, his answer was that he protected the treatments he gave by saying, "Thank God, this treatment is not going to heal anybody." If we have the idea that our treatment is going to heal someone or that spiritual power is going to remove sin or disease, we have not caught the Christ-message. The Christ-message is not that at all, although the Christ-message does use language like "heal the sick."[1] The Christ-message is a revelation of God as individual being, God as individual you and me, God as our life, mind, and soul, God even as the substance of our form, our body.

There is spiritual light; there is spiritual healing. Whether it is meditation, treatment, or prayer, the first word should be God. If a person should say to me, "I have a headache," I immediately inwardly respond with "God." The minute I say, "God,"

I know that the person cannot have a headache because God constitutes his being. If God cannot have a headache, God's being cannot have a headache, nor can the body of God, which is the temple of God, have a headache. If, on the other hand, I were to begin with a person, then I might have someone with a headache or any other mental, moral, or financial ill. But I begin with God.

Because God is individual being, there is no room for criticism or condemnation. When people come into the office of a practitioner of spiritual healing, they may tell him of the most horrible sins, but he does not react to them with condemnation or criticism. Neither does he praise them for their feelings or actions. He sees through their humanhood to God who constitutes their being. That realization wipes out both the desire and the penalty for sin. The practitioner's work is to see God as constituting individual being.

Material Laws Do Not Operate in the Presence of God Realized

Years ago a call came from a hospital in regard to a young woman who was in the delivery room. Apparently it was a breech case, with the child turned around. Every physical means was being used to turn the child around for delivery. They simply could not succeed in bringing it forth. The mother's pulse was dropping, and the doctor turned to his nurse and asked her to telephone me.

By the time the nurse got back to the delivery room, the baby had turned itself around and delivered itself, with no human hands touching it. What made the difference? I was miles away from the place, so there was no possible way for me to do anything in a human way about it. When the call came, however, just one word came to me, "God: God is the father and the mother. God is the father? Then I don't think that there is any trouble going on." That was the end of it; that was the treatment. There was no time for treatment at a later time. The treatment had to be instantaneous, which it was, and it consisted of the realization: God is the only father and God is the only mother. What can I worry about? If God is the father and God is the mother, I can't be worried about a birth or a delivery.

That ended it, and that realization of truth appeared in the physical world as normalcy and harmony. In many different cases of healing, it has been my experience that the moment the word God comes to mind the realization follows:

> God constitutes individual being.
> God is individual life.
> God is the only activity going on.

At the very instant of that realization, harmony appears. Why? Because we are neither physical healers, nor are we in competition with *materia medica*, and we never try to be. We never say that what *materia medica* does is wrong and that we are right. *Materia medica* is very right on its plane of operation, but we have nothing to do with that plane. Many of the men and women engaged in the practice of medicine are working wholly from the standpoint of matter, although the more enlightened physicians are coming to the point of introducing more and more of spiritual realization into their activity.

We are not doctors; we are not healers; we have nothing to do with modes or means of *materia medica*, nor its purpose. We are spiritual revelators of the truth that God constitutes individual being, your being and mine. Your being, therefore, is spiritual and governed by spiritual law, not material law. There are no material laws governing you once you have come out from under the law and have accepted divine grace. But you have accepted divine grace only when you have accepted God as constituting your being and mine.

When you see a sinner, you have to remain steadfast to the truth that God constitutes individual being. When you can do that, you become a successful practitioner. The success of a practitioner cannot be measured by the number of sick people made well. The true achievement is revealing individual Christhood in its perfection as individual being. On that point you will need a great deal of study, reflection, and meditation. The more intense study you give to it, the greater will be the development of your spiritual consciousness, which will ultimately enable you to be an instrument for healing without going through hours of treatments.

Forgiveness, the Evidence of a Healing Consciousness

A healing consciousness is that consciousness which prays for its enemies. How do you pray for your enemies if you do not take cognizance of error in prayer? First of all, you have to do as Jesus directed his disciples to do: put up your sword.[2] Do not use any human means of protection or retaliation, because then you are acknowledging a power apart from God. Put up your sword in the realization that "the battle is not yours, but God's."[3] You have nothing to do but stand still in the realization of God. Do not fight physically; do not fight mentally; do not wish to see vengeance heaped upon your enemies; and do not wish to see them punished. Instead take the second step, "Father, forgive them; for they know not what they do."[4]

If you are able to realize the infinite nature of your being, recognize God as constituting your being, go to the center of your being, and have an experience that all your needs are met on the outer plane, could you ever entertain the thought of stealing, cheating, lying, or defrauding? Then when you see a man in the act of stealing, what can you say other than, "Father, forgive him, he knows not what he does." If he knew that he had the allness of God at the center of his being, would he be stealing a few dollars?

How nonsensical for a person to lie, cheat, steal, or defraud for something less than what he already has, and he already has all that God has! The only reason persons lie, cheat, steal, defraud, or commit any wrong is through ignorance. If they really knew that satisfaction can be found through a God-experience, they would not be seeking satisfaction in bars, gambling halls, and other places. Do they not go to these places for the same reasons that you who are working with spiritual principles turn to a spiritual teaching? Is it not to find peace? But they have not learned to find it this way and ignorantly they try to find it in their way. It is only ignorance. It is not evil.

For years I have worked in prisons, but I have never yet met an evil man, never one, and I have met some bad ones. Through this work I was instrumental in having a man, who had been convicted of murder released and given his freedom. He came out of the prison and was given another chance in life. You may say that he did not deserve it. The Bible teaches that "though your sins be as scarlet, they shall be as white as snow,"[5] the minute the Christ has touched a person. Saul of Tarsus was also a murderer and he probably did not deserve another chance, but he was able to redeem himself and become a valuable instrument for God.

To forgive your enemies, begin first of all, by putting up your sword of antagonism against those you have called enemies, and secondly, by forgiving them in a recognition of their Christ-identity.

The Body as an Instrument

The body is a very important instrument. Those who think lightly or disparagingly about the body do not understand it. The body is a vehicle. It is an instrument given to you for your use, much in the same way that an automobile or an airplane is an instrument given to you for transportation. You are not body and you are not in your body.

You can prove the truth of that statement in just a very few minutes if you will look down at your feet and agree that those feet are not you, but that they are yours, that you possess them, that they are your instruments. Then go on up to your knees, and see again if you find yourself there. Can you not agree that those legs are yours, but they are not you? Continue on up to your waist, on up to your chest, on up to your neck, and finally on up to your head. Then lift your topmost hair and see if you can find yourself anywhere between there and the toenails. Through practicing this exercise, you will discover that you are not body and you are not in your body.

You are as eternal, as immortal, and as omnipresent as God, because God and you are one. You are pure spirit and you are not in a body. You have a body, and that body is yours for whatever purpose your body was given to you. That body is yours to use; that body is yours to enjoy; that body is yours to keep clean and pure; that body is yours for eternity.

As you pass from childhood to maturity and even when you pass from this state of existence, you will still have your body with you. It will merely have made a transition from one form to another as the child-body made a transition to the adult-body. When you understand that, you will not try to negate the body; you will not try to die out of the body, nor will you ever be content to do anything but use it as an instrument.

If you have to stoop over to pick up something, be very grateful that you have a hand with which to do it. If you have to walk to the corner, be very glad that you have feet and legs with which to walk and move you about.

When you come to an understanding of the body in that sense, you will know why it is said in scripture, "The Lord that made thee, and formed thee from the womb. . . will help thee."[6] God is the cause and creator of your body. He gives it to you in all of its intricate perfection for your use, your enjoyment, and your well-being. As you learn to respect it, to honor it, to cleanse it, to purify it, and not to defile it, you will understand that the body really is the temple of the living God.[7]

The Bible refers to flesh as "grass,"[8] impermanent, and states that "if ye live after the flesh ye shall die."[9] John explains that "the Word was made flesh."[10] So, according to the Bible there are two types of flesh. An erroneous or incorrect concept of the flesh is entertained, which is the human interpretation of it. But "the Word was made flesh and dwelt among us," means that God became flesh, so there can be nothing sinful about that, nothing evil. That is the flesh which is this body, the temple of the living God, and when you misuse it, it is because or your misinterpretation of its function in your life.

The Mind Is Not a Creative Faculty

The mind also is an instrument, just as your body is an instrument or a vehicle given to you for your use. You are not the body and you are not the mind. You have been given a body and a mind. Again I remind you that the mind is an instrument of awareness: it is not a creative instrument and cannot create your good for you. Through your mind you can become aware of a microphone and its use; you can become aware of a table and the uses of a table. But your mind did not create those things. The creative source lies deeper than the mind, what may be called your soul, or *I*, the Self, in the depth of your being. As you learn to have a listening ear, your mind will become aware of all that is.

This is very important to understand because if you could have your wish, you might believe with a deep conviction, based on your past experience, that you know what you want and that what you want is ultimately for your good. Yet if you could have that wish granted it might turn out to be the most destructive thing that ever happened to you in all your life. Over and over again, people have set their hearts or minds on a certain goal and have had no rest until they achieved it. Then when it was achieved, they found that was not what they really wanted at all. There is a part of you that knows not only what you should have but has the ability to bring it into expression for you.

When I was in business, I was seeking better business,

increased business, good business, and I got it. But I did not get it in the way in which I had set my mind. If my mind had been a creative agency, I could have created good business and would have been satisfied, but in doing so I would have lost these twenty-seven years of demonstration in spiritual work. These twenty-seven years have meant more to me than all the good business there ever was in the world.

The mind cannot know your need because that is not its purpose. Through the mind you become aware of what is necessary for you to know. You can study music with the mind; you can study law; you can study medicine; you can study metaphysics; you can study art; and through the mind you can become aware of everything already known. When you want to go beyond what is already known to the source of all wisdom and knowledge in order to discover what is required, however, the mind must become still, alert, and receptive to the flow that comes from deep within. That, you may call your soul, your real being, or your real Selfhood. Whatever name you call It, It is God, but God appearing as the son of God, as Christhood, or the spiritual son.

Trusting the Infinite Invisible

For any and every purpose, the height of demonstration is attained through stillness or silence. When you can close your eyes and be still, something wells up from within, and though It may say nothing to you, nevertheless It will open the pathway to your harmony. If you, however, believe that it is possible for you, yourself, to determine what your good is, by some fluke you may get what you are looking for, and in some cases be content or satisfied with it, but in many cases be very sorry or disappointed; whereas, in trusting the infinite invisible the experience becomes joyous, prosperous, satisfying, and fulfilling.

Although this may be very difficult in the beginning, the mode or method of it is simple when it is understood. It is a turning within somewhat in this manner:

Father, I know not how to pray
or what to pray for.
I know not how to go out or how to come in.
But You are the all knowing
infinite intelligence of this universe.
You created me from the womb.
You supplied me with all that I am,
ever have been, or ever will be.
Your grace is my sufficiency.

I can trust You, the infinite intelligence
of this universe, You who know enough to
govern the tides, the sun, the stars, the moon,
and who holds the whole rhythm of the universe in
Your hands. Your might I can trust;
Your power, Your justice, Your love.
You are the reality of my being.
You are my judge; You are my guide and
my counsel. I trust You, the infinite invisible.
I trust You, the all knowing God.
You, the all loving Father, I can trust.

I can have faith, confidence,
and assurance in the ability of
that which formed me to maintain and
sustain me in all my ways,
to direct my paths in righteousness,
to lead me "beside the still waters,"[11]
to make me "lie down in green pastures."[11]
I believe that You, the infinite intelligence of this
universe, if I heed You,
will keep me in all my ways so that
I need never come into conflict
with my brother man.

Can I look upon even this visible earth
without realizing that there is
a divine law, a divine love, a divine principle,
a divine intelligence and a divine being?
Is it not better to rely on It,
to put my whole heart and faith and
soul and trust in It rather than to
believe in the powers of my mind,
my body, my wisdom, or my integrity?
Yes, "closer. . . to me than breathing,
and nearer than hands and feet"
within me, within my consciousness,
is the source of this infinite wisdom, this divine love.

Instead of having a wish or a desire,
I surrender myself to the government
and the guidance of that which controls
the rhythm of the world,
the rhythm of the universe,
the rhythm of song and of speech.
Day by day, little by little,
I surrender myself and my life to this
infinite invisible, becoming still and listening.
I listen for Its guidance,
for Its direction,
because this guidance comes
from the universal
principle which is intelligence and
wisdom and from the love that holds everything
within Its grasp.

I will follow where It leads.
If it is to my business or profession,
I will carry on that business or profession

to the best of my ability.
I will perform whatever it entails,
trusting a greater wisdom and
a greater love than my own
to guide my hand, soul, and body.
I will perform every task that is
given me to do in the realization that
this all-knowing intelligence,
this gentle divine love, performs through
me all that is given me to do.

I acknowledge that God is,
infinite good is, spiritual vision is,
and therefore, divine direction must
inevitably be possible to all those who turn within.
"I am the vine, ye are the branches."[12]
As I, the branch, turn within to the Vine,
the Christ, the spirit of God,
or Holy Comforter within me,
It strengthens me.
It gives me greater wisdom than
my education could ever produce for me,
greater direction than all the philosophies of
the world could open up for me.

I acknowledge the Father within me as the source.
Every day I open my inner ears to Its leading,
to Its direction, to Its guiding.

Do you not see that This at the center of your being will
then take over your life and you will be able to say with Paul, "I
live; yet not I, but Christ liveth in me,"[13] or with Jesus, "I can of
mine own self do nothing.[14]. . . The Father that dwelleth in me,
he doeth the works."[15] This is the essence of their teaching.

Ask Only for Spiritual Bread

When the Master was talking to the woman at the well of Samaria, she wondered how he could give her water since he had no bucket. But he offered her a different kind of water from that found in wells: "Whosoever drinketh of the water that I shall give him shall never thirst."[16] Then the disciples came and noticed that he had had no lunch, but he said, "I have meat to eat that ye know not of."[17] Do you see that? He had meat; he had wine; he had water; he had bread; he had all of these things. Where? Within his consciousness, and out of that consciousness he could provide them with the bread and staff of life.

People have misunderstood the statement, "Ask, and it shall be given you; seek and ye shall find, knock, and it shall be opened unto you."[18] They have believed that you were to ask for a car, or as one teacher said, "Be sure it is a Cadillac and not a Ford, because God can just as easily give you a Cadillac as a Ford."

The Master never taught that you should ask for material things, seek persons, or human conditions. Throughout all his ministry he indicated that your seeking should be for the kingdom of God, for the realization or experience of God, for the wisdom and the love of God. As you keep your asking, seeking, and knocking in the area of desiring spiritual reality, recognizing that you have no need of taking thought for the things of this world, you find that this great God, this great joy at the center of your being, does have joy and great pleasure in fulfilling you, and in giving you the whole kingdom.

Take no anxious or fearful thought, but rather go within and then become aware of the infinite invisible as the source of all inspiration, all good, all activity, all life, business, art, and talents. That does not mean that you are not to take thought for your business when you are at business or that you are not to do your work to the best of your ability, or that you are not to practice your piano, your singing, or painting diligently. It does mean that you are to take no anxious thought. Having given recognition to the Infinite Invisible, you sit quietly and begin as if you were holding your ear open to hear, become attentive and receptive to the withinness.

Trusting Omniscience

This is Thy day, God. Live it for me.
This is Thy world, govern it.
I am Thy child: direct me,
lead me, instruct me.
Of myself, I am nothing,
but by the grace of Thy presence,
I have infinite capacity, infinite wisdom,
infinite guidance, and an infinity of love.

As you practice a meditation of this type, eventually there will come that experience of an inner release, a deep breath, truly a wonderful feeling. It is an assurance and a conviction that God actually is on the field. Humanly, you may not know what you are going to do when you get to the office or when you go marketing or shopping. You may have no knowledge at all of what lies ahead of you, but you do have a knowledge that you are not alone. You now have the conviction that God is consciously with you, so you need have no concern. You will not have to live your life alone and be responsible for everything that takes place; you will have divine guidance, divine wisdom, divine justice, divine love with you always, so it matters not whether you know or do not know what lies ahead.

If you should be thinking in terms of praying for a new house in the suburbs and were to give up such attempts, you might find that your fulfillment lay in moving to another city, another country, or another position. You never know what lies ahead of you when you, yourself, are not outlining your future but are permitting the grace of God to take over.

The All-Sufficiency of God's Grace

One of the most important teachings of the Infinite Way is: "My grace is sufficient for thee."[19] In accepting that as a mode of life, you are not asking for dollars, homes, or demonstrations of any kind. You realize that if you have God's grace, you have a sufficiency. God's grace is your sufficiency, and you abide in that realization. Then as if you had blinders on your eyes, you keep your vision straight ahead, looking neither this way nor that way for your life or your demonstration. You watch that spiritual grace take form in what the world calls human forms and terms of good, human avenues or channels of good.

> Thy grace is my sufficiency:
> Thy grace, Thy presence.
> All I ask in this world is a realization of Thy presence.
> Having that, I have all: having all,
> but not having that, I have nothing.

As you abide in the realization that the grace of God is your sufficiency in all things, one of these days you feel that spiritual grace within you. Then your work is prospered without your anxious and fretful human efforts.

For example, a class in a place as far from home as South Africa comes about. How? I had nothing to do with its being held there. Yet the grace of God brought this blessing to me. I did nothing about it: I did not seek it; I did not look for it; I did not pray for it; I did not do mental work about it. In fact, I had no thought about it at all. Out of the clear blue sky, it presented itself. Do you understand that? Do you see that? It is an actual truth that of all the people in those classes, in one sense I was the least responsible of all of them for the class being there. What was I responsible for? Did I have any responsibility? Yes, I was responsible years before for so living in the realization of God's grace that when the book *The Infinite Way* came through my consciousness I wrote it down. When it had to be published, it was published. That was the extent of my responsibility.

Ever since then my only responsibility has been to live every day in conscious union with God, and all these things that have happened all around the world are the externalization of my conscious communion with God. All that I am ever called on to do, and I do it unfailingly every day of the week, dozens of times in every day, is to retire within to my inner being, inner communion, and there realize my peace.

Love Seeks No Return

God's grace is my sufficiency.
God is the intelligence governing my universe,
the divine love flowing out from me and back to me.
God's love flows out from me, not my love to you.
God's love flows through me to you and
God's love through you—
not your love but God's love—
is bountiful, and that is what I seek:
God's love through you.

Personal love always ends up being selfish. Personal love always ends up wanting something for itself. But when divine love flows through you, you want nothing from anyone. When divine love flows through someone else to you, you want nothing of him. Then you are all in heaven. The moment none of us wants anything from another we are in heaven. Desire is what keeps us clamped to earth; desire is what keeps us earthbound. We loose our ties to earth when we loose desire, except the one desire, to know God. To desire to know God's grace, that is the only legitimate desire.

If by divine grace, God's love can flow through to you, it does so without any desire for a return. When God's love flows through you to me, it is not seeking a return: it is offering itself.

That is the nature of divine love that someday must be realized in families. Someday every husband must realize that his wife owes him nothing and has no obligation to him, and every wife must realize that her husband owes her nothing. Regardless of the fact that the law says he owes her a living, she must release it, and they both must come to the conclusion that they owe each other nothing but to love one another. That is enough. Then they have released themselves from every earth tie. What the husband does for the wife, he does freely out of a heart full of love and gratitude; what the wife does for the husband is done out of a free offering of self.

When children learn that they do not get their pennies for being good or doing chores, but out of love, that they are receiving their support, their education, not because of some return the parent wants, but out of the purity of parental love, the child becomes a different creature.

When a husband turns his wife loose in the realization that she belongs to God, and all that is expected of her is what God demands of her, a wholly different life comes into the household. It my be a far-off day before we see that universally, but we are all going to see it because it must come. We cannot continue to do things because there is a legal obligation, a moral obligation, or some other form of obligation. The day must come when what we do is done for love. When what we do is for love, we seek no return. That is the way God operates; that is the way God's love is. God's love flows to this universe, but it seeks no return. God does not even seek thanks or praise.

The reason we give constant praise is that we need to do that. We cannot live without praise of God, love for God, acknowledgment of God, realization of God. God does not require it. God does not even know that it is in existence, but we do, because the very emotion of praise, thanksgiving, and gratitude is a part of the quality of God-love. Life becomes very beautiful when we know that the Christ lives in us, and we follow Its inner direction.

To attain the Christ-peace and love there must be the ability to be still at least twice a day, to be silent, and to have no other desire than the desire to know God, to hear God, to realize God's grace, and to surrender ourselves to God's government. Then, when we go out into the world, we do not carry our religion on our sleeve; we do not preach; we do not proselyte; we do not force it upon anybody: we live it. If others notice it we share it liberally when they ask for it. Until they ask for it we keep our fingers on our lips. It is a strange thing that the things of God are foolishness with man. And until man is a step above being man and some trace of love has entered his heart, man does not want to know about the things of God. But when the love of God has become a conscious awareness within him, he wants to know about these things and when he does, we share them.

TAPE RECORDED EXCERPTS
Prepared by the Editor

Nuggets

"Whatever our particular work in life may be, let us undertake it in the realization that we are instruments for the activity and flow of the divine, and let It operate. Let us be sure, however, when It does, that we do not assume personal credit and personal responsibility, and that we do not go into a personal decline when we go through periods of seeming barrenness. They may not be periods of barrenness: they may be periods of rest, of further intake, like the days the Master spent away doing no mighty works."

Joel S. Goldsmith, "Fishers of Men,"
The 1953 Second Seattle Class.

Chapter Eight

Illumined Prayer

G od is at the center of our being, and in one way or another It can make Itself known to us. It may be interpreted as
sound or as light. Many persons, however, do not hear sound or
see light: they merely have a feeling of the presence. But in
whatever way It translates Itself to a person, It is an evidence of
Immanuel, God with us. Whether we hear, see, or feel something, that something is an effect, not God. It is the effect of the
invisible presence called God. I, myself, am neither clairvoyant
nor clairaudient. I have no psychic gifts whatever, and never
have had, so I have not had some of the experiences others may
have had.

Only Those of Spiritual Vision
Can Witness the Ascension

Had we been present when Jesus walked the earth after his
entombment, following the crucifixion, we might have been
one of the five hundred who saw Jesus and spoke with him, or
one of the multitudes who said that Jesus had been buried and
his friends had taken the body away, leaving the tomb empty.
Had we been one of those five hundred who saw him, we would

have been one of those of spiritual vision who became a follower of the Master. Had we been one of the multitudes who did not witness him walking the earth, we would have been one of those earthbound persons who sees only what he believes or believes only what he sees; one of those who, if he cannot see it, hear it, taste it, touch it, or smell it, does not believe. The Hebrews of those days saw only the body that was entombed; those who saw Jesus walk the earth again became the Christians.

If those of us on the three-dimensional level of life had been present with Enoch, Elijah, or Jesus, we would most likely not have been aware that they ascended or were translated because unless we had the spiritual vision of the fourth-dimensional consciousness, we would not have witnessed it. Instead we would have seen what we call a corpse or the mortal remains right where everyone else in the third-dimensional plane saw the same thing.

Elisha wanted to succeed Elijah and begged him: "I pray thee, let a double portion of thy spirit be upon me. And he said, Thou hast asked a hard thing: nevertheless, if thou see me when I am taken from thee, it shall be so unto thee."[1] What Elijah meant was "If you see me mounting up to heaven, meaning if you have the spiritual vision to see me ascending, you are a spiritual master, so you already have the cloak. I have not the power to give you my cloak. I have not the power to make you my successor. You, yourself, have the power if you have risen to the consciousness where you behold me ascend. If you do not, you will see me as a corpse here on the ground, and then you cannot be my successor because you do not have that consciousness."

Why Did Jesus Show Forth the Demonstration of Ascension to the World?

If we are looking out through the three-dimensional mind, we will not see the spiritual experience. When we are sufficiently developed spiritually, we will behold one great truth. In the entire history of the world not one person has ever died, and all that we see of sickness and death is an illusion. It is a hypnotic impression in our mind, and it is as unreal as are the snakes seen in delirium tremens. It is as much an illusion as the car tracks that come together in the distance.

There is no such thing as an externalized illusion. Either death is an illusion or God is an illusion. If there is God, there is no death. So one or the other has to be an illusion, and no one can tell us which is the illusion but our own heart. If I tell you out of my experience, there is no reason for you to believe me. But when your own heart reveals to you that there is a God and God is immortal and infinite life, then where is death? The experience of ascension is true, but it takes spiritual vision to see it.

So today, if we believe that Jesus actually walked the earth after the crucifixion, we are Christians. But if we believe that, we must go a step further: we must ask ourselves why he showed forth that demonstration to the world. Did he do it so that he might be glorified? Or did he do it to show that that is the truth about you and me? If we believe that he did it to glorify himself so that he might become the central theme of a church teaching and be worshiped as a king of God, then we have missed his whole teaching.

Over and over again Jesus said, "I can of mine own self do nothing,[2] . . . the Father that dwelleth in me, he doeth the works,"[3] your Father and my Father. His entire teaching indicated that anything he said of himself was the truth about us. "Verily, verily, I say unto you, He that believeth on me, the works that I do shall he do also; and greater works than these shall he do.[4] . . . Call no man your father upon the earth: for one is your Father which is in heaven."[5] What he was saying was that even as he called no man on earth his father, so we should call no man on earth our father.

Consciousness Forms a Perfect Body

The reason that Jesus showed forth the body after the resurrection was so that we might understand that there is no death. Man walks after death in the same body in which he walks before death. The proof of it is that Jesus showed those with eyes to see the same body with nail prints in it and with a wound in the side. It was not some kind of an ethereal or astral body. It was the body that had nail prints in it, the body that had the thrust of the knife wound in it. It was the same body with which he was entombed that he walked the earth. Then at the period of the ascension, his body was transformed into the pure vision of Spirit, which is the real body, his as well as yours and mine.

As long as there is a fleshly concept of body, we will continue to appear, even after death, in a fleshly concept of body. But the very moment that we begin to rise above the earthly concept of body, we begin to realize that our body is the temple of the living God. God created our body right from the womb; therefore, the body must be spiritual and the womb spiritual.

As that realization dawns in consciousness, our body will take on a different look and have a different feeling. No longer will it be so weary or tired; no longer will it show forth age or weakness. No longer will any of these material things happen to the body, but we will see the body and feel the body as it is in its eternal youth. That will come, however, only with a change of consciousness. It will not come by means of exercise or diet only. The greatest exponent of exercise and diet was far from an attractive looking person even though he professed to having given seventy years of his life to making his body perfect. We should be sensible about eating and exercise, but not believe that diet and exercise will make a perfect body. One thing alone will produce a perfect body, and that is our consciousness of God. Our consciousness of God will take form as a sound body, capable of meeting every demand that may be made upon it.

Human Experience Is Transformed by an Activity of Consciousness

Only a transformation of consciousness will produce a transformation of human experience. "Be ye transformed by the renewing of your mind."[6] That is the secret. When we go through a transformation of consciousness, we become renewed in body. We will make and remake our body, our purse, and our home by a transformation of consciousness, and that transformation of consciousness comes when, instead of having more faith in body, money, or demonstrations, we release all that and turn wholeheartedly to filling our consciousness with truth and keeping it filled with truth.

We must keep our mind stayed on God: abide in the Word and let the Word abide in us. Then that spiritual transition within will take place as a physical transition without. It will change the whole mode of our living: our body, our business, our home, our art, our profession. Everything will be brought under the grace of God instead of under the laws of matter or economics.

God Realized Appears as an Infinity of Good

During the years of the depression in the 1930's, the whole world was praying and fighting for supply, so much so that we could easily have imagined that there was less supply on earth than there had ever been before. People were desperate, yet all that time there were just as many vegetables in the ground, just as much fruit, just as many animals, just as many fish in the sea, just as many birds in the air, all this, while people were crowding churches to pray for supply. What foolishness, what foolishness!

Let us stop all this praying or fighting for things, and sit back in quietness and confidence, letting the infinite abundance of God, which already fills the earth, flow through us and out from us. There never was a lack, even through those ten years of the Great Depression. The lack was not because of God or because of a lack on earth. It was because of man's mismanagement of his personal and national affairs. It had nothing to do with God. God's abundance never changed or diminished during those years.

To enjoy adequate and abundant supply does not mean to pray for its increase. To enjoy supply means to bring ourselves into conscious union with God and then watch it flow into visible expression. So it is with all the other bounties: health, harmony, wholeness, completeness, perfection. There is only one way to attain them: to be transformed by the renewing of our mind, by the transforming of our consciousness. Let us not seek forms of good, but rather seek the substance of good which is the realization of God. God realized within appears as an infinity of good in the without.

Putting on the Spiritual Armor of Prayer

Our role in life is not to fight the evils in the world with the weapons of the world. "No weapon that is formed against thee shall prosper,"[7] if we do not take up the world's weapons. If we do, we may find ourselves defeated. Through Infinite Way principles we are able to put on the spiritual armor and the spiritual sword, which means prayer and meditation.

If there were an evil threatening this world in any form, I would count it a great blessing to retire from public lecturing, teaching, and writing, go off into the hills somewhere and pray, and put into active operation what I have learned in the Infinite Way. Through prayer I have already discovered that any form of evil there is on earth can be overcome, but I have learned, also, that the only way it can be overcome is through prayer.

The Healing of the Nations

This would not be true, of course, to those who know nothing of illumined prayer. I do not refer to the prayer that is taught in churches. Such prayer has been going on for dozens of centuries, but it has not yet brought freedom to the world at large. But prayer, according to the Infinite Way, which is a conscious union with God, a conscious God-contact, does result in the overcoming of every form of discord: personal, family, community, national, and international. We will not see evidence of that on a large scale. In fact, it has not been tried on a large scale, because there are not too many people in the world who know what effectual prayer is.

As indicated in scripture, those who know the meaning of prayer, the "ten"[8] righteous men can save a city. A few persons, understanding that prayer means an actual contact with God and sitting in the silence until that God-contact is realized, can overcome all the discords of earth, for themselves individually, for the family group, for the community, and ultimately nationally and internationally.

Up to this point, everyone who has been engaged in any metaphysical or spiritual activity has seen the truth of this in individual healings: the evils of disease, sin, and of false appetite overcome. That has been going on for the past one hundred years through the many schools of metaphysical teachings that have sprung up.

The Far Reaching Effects of God-Realization

Illumined prayer, which means the conscious realization of God, does result in the overcoming of sin, disease, lack, and limitation for individual you and me. In those families where this form of understanding prayer or truth is known, the health of family life is improved, not only physically, but mentally and morally. Where a mother is governing her household through illumined prayer, there is a minimum of juvenile delinquency and of childhood diseases. That has been apparent for years and years in this work.

In my personal experience, I have witnessed the larger proof of this work in capital and labor experiences and in corporation and union activities. I have seen that where one group—in some cases capital and in other cases labor—was willing to rely on spiritual prayer and abide by it, harmony has resulted without the use of force and with a joyous solution for everyone concerned.

I have also witnessed it in some of the affairs concerning our government where on occasions when it looked as if serious evils were about to befall the country, the power of this conscious realization of God resulted in the overcoming of that experience. It was not asking God to do something, not asking God to stop something, not trying to be wiser than God. It was acknowledging that God is the infinite intelligence of the universe, but then giving It an outlet into this universe so that It could operate. The presence and power of God is here and It is now, but It can function only through consciousness. If there had been no Jesus, there would have been no such teaching as the Master's, although God was there and the teaching was there. But had there been no Jesus, there would have been no avenue through which it could have been admitted to human experience.

Always the presence and power of God has filled the earth, but it took a Moses to bring manna from the sky, see the Red Sea open, and lead the Hebrews out of slavery into freedom. Why Moses? Moses was the man who stood still and realized the presence of God, and in the realization of the presence of God, God could operate in human experience. Isaiah, Elijah, Elisha, Daniel, Joel, all these men were instruments of God who opened their consciousness so that God could flow through them into experience and bless this world.

Then came the Master, Christ Jesus, who did the same thing on a much greater scale. He admitted frankly that he could of his own self do nothing, but he opened his consciousness to let the Father come through and multiply loaves and fishes, heal the sick, and raise the dead. He never claimed to do these things himself: he merely stood silently in conscious contact with the Father, and then the Father could flow through him. Every spiritual practitioner today must admit that he does not know how to heal or what it is that heals or how healing is accomplished.

The Illumined Prayer of Conscious Contact

Prayer has nothing to do with asking God for something. Prayer has nothing to do with expecting something from God. Prayer has to do with making a conscious contact with God, and eventually conscious union, so that we can actually feel that God is on the field. God, being the infinite intelligence of the universe, can be trusted to do whatever is necessary in Its own way. It raises up seed wherever necessary to perform any function.

If we can see that the nature of prayer really means contacting God to make a way for God's glory to escape from within so that It can perform the functions of healing the sick and raising the dead, then we will understand the nature of God and the nature of prayer. The nature of God is infinite intelligence and divine love. Therefore, we never have to tell God anything, advise God, or influence God, because God is already infinite intelligence. We need never ask anything of God because God is divine love and, as the Master has told us, "It is your Father's good pleasure to give you the kingdom,"[9] not have us ask for it, beg for it, or plead for it.

Knowing this enables us to turn from that form of outmoded prayer to the illumined prayer which is a conscious contact with God so that we actually feel the presence, feel the release and the assurance, and then we can go about our business, because now we have the greatest wisdom of all working in us, through us, and for us. We have the divine love of this universe working in us, through us, and for us. But without a conscious contact, a realization, or the experience of God, we have nothing more than a blind faith in something that more often than not will disappoint us.

As we make our conscious communion with God and have the God-experience, as we feel the very presence, power, and joy of the Spirit, our external affairs will change, and then we will know why James said, "Ye ask, and receive not, because ye ask amiss."[10] If the world could recognize that, it would change its mode and form of prayer, and then it would realize what God really is. God is, be assured of that, and God is a saving grace, but there must be God, not talk about God.

The Prayer of Communion Awakens Our Relatives and Friends

To reach the consciousness of a member of the household who is not merely unresponsive and unreceptive but actually antagonistic to all things spiritual, a person should pray the prayer of communion, that is, try to turn the whole situation over to God:

God, I do not know how to pray.
I do not know what to pray for.
I have no power to transform human consciousness.
All I know is that all power is
in the Infinite Invisible.

Then as he is still and a feeling of release and of God's presence comes, if there is a trace of receptivity in that person, he will respond to it. If not, he will have to continue on his human way until he awakens of his own accord.

No one can bring all of his relatives and friends to God, and this always has been true. Jesus could not even bring his mother, his brothers, or his sister. Of his mother Jesus said, "Who is my mother? and who are my brethren? And he stretched forth his hand toward his disciples, and said, Behold my mother and my brethren!"[11]

Many in this work find that their relatives or friends are

unwilling to follow in this path so they have to leave them alone to follow their own way. Just as we would not want anyone to interfere with our following our way of life, so we must not interfere with someone else's following his way of life, even though he may temporarily come on some evil days. Those very evil days may eventually be his salvation. We cannot drive a person to heaven, although sometimes his troubles do. All we can do is to pray the prayer of communion, turn the whole situation loose, let God do Its work, and if a person is ready for the experience he will awaken to it, and if not then we will have to go our way and let him go his. That does not mean breaking up households. It just means living our own life internally and letting others live their own live.

Witnessing
Reincarnation Here and Now

Reincarnation, as it is usually understood, is the concept that people who die are reborn again. We, however, have come to the knowledge that no one ever dies, so he cannot be reborn. Many of us have witnessed reincarnation here and now in that in our own live we have lived many lives. For example, I lived twenty-two years as a businessman, and that was one life. I died to that man and was reborn as a healer or practitioner. For sixteen years I did nothing but sit in an office and do healing work. Then evidently I died again and was reborn into the Infinite Way. Healing, teaching, lecturing, and revealing a spiritual way of life became a whole new life for me.

When I died to the business world, everybody in that world died away from me, that is, dropped out of my experience. Not one individual came over from my social or business life into my Christian Science life. When I died to the Christian Science life, ninety-nine out of one hundred people that I knew in Christian Science died, too, so far as I was concerned and did not come into the Infinite Way life. So the Infinite Way life has been a whole new birth. Most of those who were with me in my Christian Science life, with the exception of perhaps a few dozen people, did not come into my new life.

And who is to say that I am not going to have a fourth life, and a fifth one, and a sixth one? I am positive that I will die to this particular activity of lecturing, teaching, and healing and will then find myself living a life on a different plane of consciousness, although I may still be here and be visible, or I may depart and be invisible, but in either case I am going to die again and be reborn again. Probably many of those who are with me today will die away from me so that in my next life, whatever form it may be, here on earth or in the next plane, I may have to find a whole new circle of friends and co-workers. I do not know and you do not know.

Everyone dies. We died to our early years: to rattles and toys; later we died to schoolbooks. We have also died out of one life after another and been reborn into a higher form of life. Some have died out of youth into parenthood, a different life from the earlier life. We are always dying and we are always being reborn, but we never die in the sense of the world's meaning of death. We never experience death; we never experience extinction. Just as we pass from childhood to youth, youth to parenthood, and parenthood to the present stage of development, so we pass from glory to glory, each state higher than the other. We can never experience death, although some day we will experience passing from the visible scene to the invisible, but we will quickly find that it is not death.

What It Means to
Dwell in the Secret Place

The answer to every discord on earth is in scripture. We can begin with the 91st Psalm: "He that dwelleth in the secret place of the most High shall abide under the shadow of the Almighty,"[12] and none of the evils of the world will come nigh his dwelling place. We have not lived "in the secret place of the most High." We may have gone to church on Sunday, but that hardly constitutes living "in the secret place of the most High." We may have done some ushering or some committee work, too, but that does not constitute living "in the secret place of the most High."

Living "in the secret place of the most High" means dwelling there, abiding there, remaining there, living forever in the consciousness of God, praying without ceasing, keeping our mind stayed on God. "In all thy ways acknowledge him, and he shall direct thy paths."[13] We experience discords on earth because we do not live "in the secret place of the most High." Jesus the Christ tells us that in the 15th Chapter of John: "I am the vine, ye are the branches. He that abideth in me, and I in him, the same bringeth forth much fruit. . . . If a man abide not in me, he is cast forth as a branch, and is withered."[14] And that is the only answer there is to discord in our experience.

Scripture also states, "I have been young, and now am old; yet have I not seen the righteous forsaken, nor his seed begging bread."[15] Who are the righteous? Those who live and move and have their being in God consciousness, those who pray without ceasing, those who live in constant communion with God, those who dwell "in the secret place of the most High," those who make God their hiding place, their high tower, their fortress. A thousand may still fall at our left hand, and ten thousand at our right hand, but it will not come nigh us. And as that thousand and ten thousand begin to abide in God, the evils will not come nigh them.

In this connection I am reminded of a period when there was a polio epidemic. On the front page of a newspaper, there was an article about a child who died of polio while under prayer treatment, whose life, the newspaper indicated surely could have been spared had the parents called medical aid. I called the editor of that paper and thanked him for the article and for putting it on the front page.

He was surprised, "Why should you thank me?"

"Well," I said, "I am interested in spiritual healing and spiritual prayer, and for that reason I am grateful that that article appeared in your paper."

"Why should you be grateful? I certainly was not complimentary to the idea."

"Yes, but you were. You paid us the greatest honor, the greatest tribute that has ever appeared in print in America."

"What are you talking about?"

"Didn't you put on the front page of your newspaper an article that a child died under prayer treatment? You must have considered that important news. It hasn't happened very often then has it, because if it happened often you would not have put it on the front page."

"Goodness," he said, "I didn't mean it that way."

"Certainly, you didn't mean it that way. You didn't know that you were calling the attention of the whole world to the fact that here was an unusual case."

He said, "I am going to do some investigating about that!"

He called me back in a few days and said, "You know, I cannot find another case of a child who died of polio under prayer treatment."

It was sad for that one child to pass on, but just think how important it is to have brought to our attention how few children do pass on under prayer treatment. When it happens it has to be front page news.

There is less disease, less sin, and less poverty in those households which rely on some kind of metaphysical teaching. The more we learn of the nature of God, the more enlightened prayer we learn, and the more we live in communion with God, the less of earthly evils will come nigh our dwelling place, until we will live in such conscious communion with God that God will constitute our entire being, and there will be no discord. Is it not clear that it is only through the example of students of spiritual wisdom that the rest of the world can be saved?

The Infinite Way Is an Unorganized Activity

Because the Infinite Way has no organization, those who adopt its principles do not have to change their religious affiliation. It is surprising how many ministers of different denominations are studying Infinite Way writings, and also how many metaphysical practitioners of all schools are bringing this message into their experience. Some of them openly acknowledge it and some do not. Whether they do or whether they do not is their own demonstration.

I have no Infinite Way as an organization to promote: I have only an infinite way of life to introduce to the world. Should I depart from this visible scene, I am leaving behind me no organization to which anyone will have to belong or owe allegiance. I have no reason to pile up any form of treasure where "moth and rust doth corrupt,"[16] more particularly organizational treasure. The present status of the Infinite Way and the status that will be in the hands of those who will administer it is this: the Infinite Way message is presented in its books and its tape recordings. They are available to the public or to anybody who cares to buy them, and they have the opportunity to live the principles set forth in whatever degree they desire. My part is finished when I have presented the message to the world and done whatever personal teaching I could do along the way. After that it depends upon the world's receptivity and responsiveness to the work, but more particularly on the example that students of the Infinite Way are able to present.

There is no provision for authorizing practitioners or teachers in the Infinite Way. No one can secure an appointment or a legalization as a practitioner or a teacher. I have no such power. I cannot make anyone a healer. If a person has the healing and teaching consciousness, he is an instrument for spiritual healing and a teacher. I cannot prevent him from being one. But, if he does not have that consciousness, I cannot make him a practitioner or teacher.

In most metaphysical teachings, it is possible to get a degree or a license by passing an examination and answering certain questions, but because a person can memorize facts in a book does not mean that he has attained the healing consciousness. Every year thousands of persons become practitioners and at the end of the year just about as many leave the practice as entered it. Why? Because they think that a certificate gives them the status of a practitioner, teacher, or leader, and that people are going to pour into their offices and be grateful enough to make it a lucrative business.

For two hundred dollars I could incorporate and give degrees to everybody in my classes, and then I could sell those titles for a specified sum of money. Those are some of the temptations that students are going to face when I am not around to stop them. That is a bad way to carry on a spiritual ministry, a very bad way. Neither I nor anyone else can appoint a person to be a practitioner or teacher in the Infinite Way.

Since the beginning of the Infinite Way, three persons who thought they were very sincere students have come to me and wanted to take over my work when I had to go on to other cities. So I introduced them and announced that in my absence they would take over. In one case, in six months it was ended, in another case eight months, and in the third case three years. But the work of all three sooner or later ended. Why? Because they did not have the consciousness to hold on to what had been given them. They did not have the consciousness to increase it. So now I do not appoint anyone or introduce anyone as my successor. If a person has the consciousness, however, his work will prosper.

If our students are strong enough never to permit anyone to organize this activity, never to permit anyone to make him a member of anything, never permit him to swear allegiance to anything, if they can be that steadfast in realizing that the intent of this message is to reveal a way of prayer, reveal a God that does not have to be prayed to, but whom one reaches in prayer and communion, then this work will have performed its function. Whatever benefit those who are in the Infinite Way can show forth will in that degree encourage others to learn how to pray the prayer of communion, how to accept a God who is an infinite intelligence and a divine love. We will not have to pray the prayer of petition any more. Our whole prayer will be a means of contact with God, a means of receiving It, experiencing It, and responding to It.

Angels

"For he shall give his angels charge over thee, to keep thee in all thy ways."[17] The angels of God may appear to us in infinite form and variety. Though I may not look it at this minute, I am an angel of God in your experience. Although our students know that I have no wings on my shoulders, I do have a well developed pair of wings on my heels. A book may be an angel in our experience, bringing us the good tidings, or it may be an actual inspiration that takes place within ourselves that is not dependent on any external means. There are times when we may call that inner inspiration an angel. It may even seem that it is a guiding angel, or a guarding, benevolent, or protecting angel.

The Holy Ghost is the communion between our human and spiritual nature, which we call God, and that communion, or Holy Ghost, is an intermediary or an angel. So in many different ways we can say that God sent an angel to us. It may have been a neighbor who came in and prayed for us; it may have been a neighbor who came in and gave us a book or a pamphlet or in some other way we were brought into a higher approach to life, and that neighbor was our angel.

Until we have received the assurance within us, our prayer has not been completed, and we should not expect too much of it. It is only when whatever knowing of the truth we do, silently or orally, is followed by a period of silent receptivity, in which we let this feeling of assurance and confidence come, that we have prayed aright and have been in communion with God. Then we can say to ourselves, "God is on the field. I can rest."

Chapter Nine

The Inner Meaning of Living the Spiritual Life

There is a way to train ourselves to practice the presence of God, a simple way that everyone can practice. It is a way that has great possibilities, and yet it is so simple that it can be taught to a six year old child.

When the telephone bell rings, most persons pick up the receiver and automatically say, "Hello." If we change that method of answering the telephone, pick up the receiver, wait a second, and then say, "Hello," very quickly, we will begin to see the miracles come into our life. In this brief pause, followed by "Hello," we have waited for the Christ to enter. If we do not do this, we are on the telephone, and the one calling is at the other end of the line. There are two human beings, who may be friendly or unfriendly, or beginning in a friendly way and possibly ending up quarreling.

But the moment that we learn to pick up the receiver, pause, admit the Christ, and then speak, there are three of us: the person making the call, the person called, and the Christ. The presence of that Christ raises the whole of human experience and makes it a spiritual one. Out of two human beings, it makes two spiritual beings. Out of possible misunderstanding, it makes for understanding. Out of incompatibility, it makes for compatibility, harmony, and peace.

Fruitage of Conscious
Remembrance of the Presence

We follow the practice of the presence in every detail of our lives: sitting down to breakfast in the morning and never touching any food until the blink of the eye, that momentary pause which admits and acknowledges the Christ; never crossing the doorstep to leave home without touching the knob of the door and then waiting that second for the Christ to go before; never going through a doorway into a building without a momentary pause which admits the Christ before us; never going marketing, shopping, or up to a counter to buy anything, or never sitting down in a restaurant without that momentary pause.

It changes all relationships because, instead of two persons facing each other as human beings, that invisible, intangible presence, this transcendental being called the Christ, the spirit of God, or the comforter enters our relationship and transforms the relationship. It transforms the relationship between buyers and salespeople, between employers and employees, between teachers and students. It changes the entire aspect of one's life, and it not only operates as a leveler in all of our relationships, but when we pause for the admission of the Christ we no longer depend on our human wisdom. That pause lets in spiritual guidance. We make no decisions: we wait for that spiritual guidance. We do not open our mouths to speak without waiting to be aware of that spiritual presence.

No activity of the day can be neglected, although at first I am frank to admit that three-quarters of them are neglected the first few days. Then we remember, "Oh, I forgot the last time," and we begin all over again. That is all right; there is no harm done. The important thing is that we begin, and every time we forget to admit the Christ then we redouble our efforts to remember It the next time, until the day comes when it is not so much a conscious effort as an almost involuntary response. It is done automatically without conscious thinking, like driving a car and then afterward wondering how it is that we drove it when we could not remember shifting gears or going through the motions of driving. Yet it all took place.

If we lean unto our own understanding, then we have the usual experience of good and evil. But if in all things we acknowledge the divine presence, then we have the aid of that spiritual entity called the Christ. There is no better way to begin such a program of training than with the telephone. With that pause before the "Hello," the Christ has come between us. It becomes a contact within us and a gentleness that may not have been there before, or it makes us more understanding or more patient.

Acknowledging God in All Our Ways

When Paul said, "I live; yet not I, but Christ liveth in me,"[1] what he meant was: I do not walk through doorways: the Christ walks through before me to greet me on the other side. I do not digest food: the Christ goes before me to digest it. I do not buy and I do not sell: the Christ goes before me.

"He performeth the thing that is appointed for me.[2]. . . The Lord will perfect that which concerneth me."[3] How can He do it if we do not admit Him into our experience? There is no He unless we ourselves admit that He into this relationship: there are just two, you and I. If one of us admits this transcendental presence into the relationship, then harmony can prevail. This is called practicing the presence of God. It really means acknowledging the presence of God in all our ways.

We acknowledge that there is more to our relationship than human good. Between us there exists a spiritual bond that unites us in oneness in God. We are not only blessing ourselves: we are blessing every individual we contact during the day because we are bringing the Christ into his experience even while he himself does not know what this spiritual power is. Very often people will say, "What is it that you have that we do not have? What is it? What is it that your group has that others do not have?" We might give a dozen different explanations, but there is only one true explanation, and that is that we have the transcendental spiritual invisible presence and power always operating in us, through us, for us, as us, as our very daily experience.

God Enters Our Experience Through Consciousness

God is and God fills this room, but that God is available to you and to me only in proportion as we open our consciousness to It. Otherwise, It can be in this room, can even be sitting on our lap, but It will bring no benefit to us, because nothing can come into our experience except through an activity of our consciousness. In other words, our body cannot admit anything to us, not our eyes or our ears. There has to be consciousness before any part of the body functions, and in the absence of consciousness there is nothing except a corpse.

Just as we cannot study music, art, literature, or mathematics except through our consciousness, because these can enter our experience only through our consciousness, so it is with God. God is available, but the Master said, "Having eyes, see ye not? and having ears, hear ye not?"[4] In other words, can we admit into our consciousness, into our inner vision, this thing called God, or are we blind to Its presence? Are we deaf to Its presence? The answer for most of us most of the time is, "Yes." We are not listening and we are not looking for It. We are so busy going ahead with what we are doing and how we are doing it that we leave no room for the transcendental and invisible presence and power that can transform our life.

If any benefit is to enter our experience, it must enter through an activity of our consciousness, and if we hope eventually to be guided by the "still small voice,"[5] to be led, to be directed by infinite intelligence, we, through an act of consciousness, must open our eyes and ears to that Infinite

Invisible. That must become a daily practice, and I do not mean once a day. I mean a daily practice all the day long. It is very difficult at first. We are accustomed to jumping out of bed, into the shower or tub, into our clothes, then down to breakfast, and off to the office. This will not do in the spiritual world or in living the spiritual life. In the time between getting out of bed and leaving for work, there should already have been twelve opportunities for opening that ear for the realization of the presence of the Christ. How many hundred times must it happen during the day until that day comes when it is no longer a conscious activity! Instead it is something that takes place as automatically as our digestion.

What Does It Mean to "Leave It to God"?

Let us never believe for a moment that we really and truly are leaving anything to God just by saying, "Oh, I am leaving it to God," because we are not. If we really were, it would always be done perfectly. No, very seldom are we leaving it to God when we say that we are leaving it to Him. We are just evading the issue and hoping it will come out right and justify us. Actually we can truthfully say, "I am leaving it to God" when we have come to the place where thirty, forty, fifty times a day we actually do open our consciousness and say, "All right, Father, You take over."

When every time we blink the eye in recognition of the activity or the presence of the Christ, then we can say, "I have turned it over to God." But it is nonsense to believe that only about once a week we can turn something over to God. We cannot. There is no God waiting. God is on the scene only in proportion as we consciously open our consciousness to Its activity. Otherwise, we are living under the law, instead of under Grace. Without the opening of consciousness to God or the realization of the Christ, we are living under the law, leaning only unto our own understanding or trying to navigate our life alone, and we may be affected by weather, we may slip in the bathtub, our car may run into a telegraph pole, or any one of a thousand things that happen to human beings can come nigh our dwelling place.

Letting the Christ Live Our Life

From the moment that we decide to admit the Christ into our relationships with everyone on earth, admit the Christ into our mealtime, our business life, home life, marketing, shopping life, we move out from under the law and begin to live under Grace. Why under Grace? Because having admitted the Christ, the Christ is always going before us to "make the crooked places straight."[6] The Christ is always walking beside us as protection, although actually there is nothing to be protected from. In the realization of this Christ, the discords and inharmonies of human experience evaporate. We live under Grace when we live through the spirit of the Christ. Paul gave it to us in these words, "I can do all things through Christ which strengtheneth me."[7]

Before beginning a class, I always open myself to the activity of the Christ. Then I can be assured that the class will be well taken care of because the Christ has been admitted to care for it, not my memory of something that I knew yesterday, not my memory of something I have read or written. Whatever the presence of God wishes to deliver will come through if I have admitted the Christ into the experience. It will not come through if I try to live by memory or by what I have known or read before.

When we rely on our own understanding, judgment, or capacity, we may have success or failure in our business transactions, and sometimes the failures will outweigh the successes. But whether or not we have nothing but success, we will not know the complete satisfaction and permanence that comes by admitting the Christ into our experience, because then under all conditions and circumstances we can rest in peace, knowing that the invisible God is on the scene.

Attaining Continuous Conscious Awareness of the Presence

We meet every situation in our experience with some spiritual or scriptural passage. We may have something to do tomorrow that at first thought looks like a hard job or even beyond us, too difficult to tackle or requiring too much of us. We are taught to turn within for some spiritual or scriptural passage that will help us meet that situation. With an assurance such as, "He performeth the thing that is appointed for me" or "The Lord will perfect that which concerneth me," we are able to drop our responsibility, because we have admitted God, the Christ, into our experience.

Let us suppose we are facing some situation where more money is demanded of us than we think we have or can afford to use, something requiring more strength than we think we have, or something requiring more patience, more kindness, more tolerance, or more forgiveness. Something more is going to be demanded of us than we feel we have, so we turn to another biblical passage and remember, "My grace is sufficient for thee,"[8] and we will meet this situation not with money, with strength, or with advice, but with God's grace.

The secret of spiritual living consists in the ability to attain the consciousness of this invisible presence until It becomes so alive and so real in us that It is as real as our right hand, as real as our checkbook or pocketbook, as real as anything in the physical realm. Those who attain this realization always have the awareness of an abiding presence. It appears in different ways, and each one realizes it in some different way, but always there is an assurance that there is something more here than we are immediately aware of. That something else is an invisible power and presence, the Christ, the spirit of God, the Comforter. We cannot have It and not know It. It always makes Itself known. But we prepare the way for Its entrance and we prepare the way for Its operation in our experience through our daily practice.

Seeking Spiritual Guidance

When we are turning within for spiritual guidance, whether a problem concerning business, finance, sales, invention, manufacturing, or family, we sit back, turn away from that problem, and open our consciousness specifically for a realization of God's presence. We cannot turn to God and say, "Where will I get a bank loan?" or, "Should I go out of business or stay in business?" That is making a human counselor out of Spirit.

The problem may try to intrude itself into our thoughts, and we will have to talk back to it, "Get thee behind me, Satan. I am not interested in you. My function now is to realize God's presence." And we will go about achieving the realization of God's presence. Whether we achieve the realization of that presence the first time we try is not the criterion.

If we continue to practice, eventually we will attain the ability to sit down and come into an actual realization of the presence of God. When we have that, we will either very quickly see the solution to our problem, or we will be led to go to a ball game, or if it is night, to go to bed. If it is the latter, we may wake up in the middle of the night or early in the morning with the solution as plain as if it were written on the ceiling. Or, we may turn away, throw it out of our mind, and then in a moment that we know not, the answer will flash right back in. We may find ourselves sitting down quietly with a pen and pencil and we will begin to write and think about our problem, not with concern or anxiety, but to let the solution flow, not from us or from our understanding, but from the contact that we have made with the divine.

We do not sit on cloud nine and deny that we are living out

from a human experience, nor do we try to avoid problems or evade situations, but we try not to tackle their solution until we have the realization of God as our partner. There is no escapism in that, because we are not trying to avoid the issues of life. What we are trying to do is not to deal with them until we are sure that we have the spirit of God working in us and through us and with us in all our ways. Once we have the assurance that God is on the field, then we sit down and map out our campaign or whatever the solution.

Always Choose the Most Competent Person for the Job

In dealing with everyday problems, it should be understood that we never go to a dentist or to a lawyer just because he is a truth-student. Many times such a person is expecting God to do his work and he just sits by and knows the truth. It is wisdom to go to a professional person who is experienced in his business. If he is an attorney, he should be thorough and look into every phase of the work. If he is a dentist, we want to be sure that he is a dentist who is not depending on God to do his sterilization work for him.

With the spirit of God at the helm, we are very thorough workmen; we leave nothing to chance; we leave nothing to "Oh, just trust God, and He will do it." Our attitude is that before we undertake anything we make sure that we have attained some realization of the presence of God and then we sit down and do a thorough job of whatever it is we are doing. I have heard women say that they do not want maids in their homes who are truth-students because they do too much praying and too little dusting. Of course, that is not always true, but there is just enough truth in such a statement for it to have some validity.

When a person is spiritually endowed and is really touched by the Spirit, he becomes a very thorough workman, leaving nothing to chance. The Spirit, Itself, drives him to go to the right place for information, to find the right people to help him, and nothing is left just to chance or to a let-God-do-it attitude. Spiritual living does not result in frustration, and it is not escapism. It is the most practical way of living in a practical universe that we can possibly know because when we have attained the ability to live through the realization of the Christ and have It with us on all occasions, we discover how practical it is in helping us meet our obligations, keep our body well, and our home in order.

Right Ambition

The spiritual life is a very practical one. It permits us to have no desires except God's fulfillment as us. If we desire to be a businessman, when we should be a professional man or in some artistic field, we may thwart our life plan. But if we perform the everyday duties that are given us to do, if we in our prayers and communion turn to the Father within in the sense of "Reveal the plan for me; reveal my purpose in life," while continuing to do what we are now doing and yet praying an inner prayer for guidance, the way will open to lead us out of what we are doing into what we should be doing. That does not mean giving up ambition. On the contrary, it is indicative of the fact that we are ambitious to be fulfilled in the sense of God fulfilling Itself, and to see ourselves functioning according to a divine order.

When I speak of desire and ambition, I am speaking of the false sense of these that lead men to become dictators or into positions in and out of government, in and out of business that will take them into high places without due regard and consideration for the rights of the world. False ambition, I consider erroneous and not a right ambition. Certainly, however, it is a right ambition to be successful. It would be a wrong ambition, however, to be successful merely in order to acquire a million dollars. So it is necessary to understand what is meant by desire and ambition. It is right to desire the realization of God. It is right to desire that God fulfill Itself as harmony in our daily living, but to go to God in prayer with a specific desire which we want God to fulfill results in failure because God does not fulfill our desires: God fulfills Itself as us.

Any prayer for increased ability to realize God, increased ability to love and to realize truth, is a legitimate form of prayer, as is any desire or request of a spiritual nature.

Spiritual Sustenance

In the Lord's Prayer, Jesus asked, "Give us this day our daily bread."[9] Was he really asking for bread? If we study the teaching of the Master, it is plain that when he said, "I am the bread of life,"[10] he was not talking about a loaf of baker's bread. He was talking about the spiritual sustenance of life, and so when he prayed, "Give us this day our daily bread," he was actually praying, "Give us this day, Father, the realization of Thy presence. Give us the conscious realization of spiritual substance. Open our eyes to the presence of divine grace."

When Jesus said, "I have meat to eat that ye know not of,"[11] he certainly was not talking about meat from a butcher shop. He was talking about meat, the spiritual substance of life, the spiritual food. When we have enough of that, we require much less of material food. We can often miss meals and not really miss them, or cut our food in half if we have enough spiritual bread and spiritual meat.

When Jesus said to the woman at the well of Samaria, "Whosoever drinketh of the water that I shall give him shall never thirst; but the water that I shall give him shall be in him a well springing up into everlasting life,"[12] he did not need a bucket to get it, because he had the water within his own being. That water was not material. The "bread, meat, wine, and water" to which the Master referred was the activity and substance of God, the life of God, and the love of God. When we talk about the blood of Jesus, we are not speaking about red and white corpuscles: we are speaking about that immortal sense of life that Jesus so well knew, and in that sense we are speaking correctly.

To pray without any desire or ambition means not to take into our prayer material desire and material ambition, but to open ourselves for the realization of God's grace. "My grace is sufficient for thee" in all things, and that Grace means bread, meat, wine, water, housing, clothing, transportation, wholeness. God's grace is our sufficiency in all things. It does not make any difference what department of life, we have only one thing to pray for: God's grace, and God's grace means God's presence:

> Thy presence is my sufficiency;
> Thy power is my sufficiency;
> Thy substance is my sufficiency;
> Thy wisdom is my sufficiency;
> Thy love is my sufficiency.

Go to God for What God Has to Give

As long as we understand that God is spirit, we must go to God only for spiritual things. That is what the Master meant when he said, "The hour cometh, when ye shall neither in this mountain, nor yet at Jerusalem, worship the Father."[13] The temple in Jerusalem was considered so holy that the Hebrews went there once a year to pray and to bring their offerings in order to attain God's blessing. "The hour cometh, and now is, when the true worshipers shall worship the Father in spirit and in truth." Jesus taught that the Father loves those who worship him in spirit and in truth, not in temples, not in holy mountains, but in spirit and in truth. That is virtually the same thing as saying that in worshiping or praying to God, we should not pray for material things because God is spirit. What we should do is pray in spirit and in truth, pray for the revelation of truth, pray for the revelation and unfoldment of spirit, pray for a realization of the presence of God. Then what? All these things will be added unto us: food, raiment, housing. All these things will be added unto us if we pray for spiritual things.

Only God's Thoughts Are Power

Many persons believe that thinking good thoughts is a form of prayer, that they are conceived in God-consciousness and imbued with spiritual power. If good thoughts were spiritual power, however, no parent on earth would lose a child and few children would ever lose a parent. Spiritual power is an emanation of God, and it operates with or without thoughts. Thoughts are not necessary to spiritual power. As a matter of fact, silence is the deepest and greatest spiritual power. When we are deepest in the silence, there is more of spiritual power evident than with speech. Has it not been said that speech is silver and silence is golden?

When we can put the finger on the lips and are absolutely silent, the presence and power of God comes through. Then we may voice some thought that comes to us as a result of that God-experience, but the words we voice or the thoughts we think are not the power. It is the consciousness of God that is the power. We may say, "God bless you"; "Safe journey"; "I wish you Godspeed"; or "The best of everything to you." But how meaningless that is except as a form of courtesy between us! It is nothing more or less than our human good wishes for one another, and they are not power.

Power is the presence of God. If we take our friends into our consciousness in silence, we give them a greater degree of God-speed than all the words that were ever thought, spoken, or written. When we are depending on good thoughts, we are depending on effects, and effects can never be God. No matter how good the thoughts are, they are effects. The power is in the consciousness from which good thoughts emanate.

How many persons express good thoughts to us today and turn around tomorrow and express the very opposite? That that is possible shows that they were not God's thoughts, because nobody could express a God-thought today and then express an evil one tomorrow. In God there are not the pairs of opposites called good and evil. Let us not depend on good thoughts but on an actual realization of God's presence.

The statements of truth that we use when we go into our meditation are only a preparation for the experience of the God-presence and God-power. We do not depend on those statements or thoughts of truth that we are thinking, except to help us go deeper into the silence. Then in the silence, the presence and power of God reveals Itself.

Truth Voiced Out of the Mind Is Not Power

When some metaphysicians are called upon for help they immediately answer with what can be called clichés: "Oh, it isn't true"; "There are no accidents in divine love"; "Pain isn't real." It is as if they believed that uttering such things had power. As far as I am concerned, they have power only to make me angry, because when an individual knows the truth or has the consciousness of those statements, he does not make such statements. He just says, "Very well, I will be with you right away." Then the patient can feel the power because he really does know that there is no reality to the claim.

When truth is voiced out of the mind, it is not power. If it were power all the people who learned truth out of books and who repeat statements of truth would be doing healing work. But all the good thoughts they can think and the good things they can remember from books are not healing power. If entertained in thought sufficiently, however, they can lead one deep enough into the silence so that the real power will come through.

Always remember that an effect is not power. Somebody at one time told a person just to hold a Bible in his hand, and he would get healed. Why? Does the printed word in the Bible have power? It is when we read the printed word and it awakens or arouses something in us that the power is there, but not until then.

If we are helping someone, and a spiritual truth pops into our head, there can be a remarkable healing. Then tomorrow somebody may ask us for help, and we will think of that truth and repeat it, and nothing will happen. And we will wonder why. The reason is that we cannot live on yesterday's manna, and the truth that was effective yesterday is not necessarily effective today because it did not come from the same source. When that word of truth comes to us from the depth of our withinness, it is from God. "The word of God is quick, and powerful, and sharper than any two-edged sword."[15] It does not say anything about the power of your word or mine. It says, "The word of God is quick, and powerful, and sharper," and so it is.

The Word Is Sharp and Powerful

If we can be silent and receptive, if we can be still and listen, and the Word jumps out, then we should not be surprised if the dead walk, because the word of God is that powerful. But if it is not the word of God, we cannot expect too much from it, because it never has been promised that you or I could do anything with our right thinking. The Master covered that point too, didn't he, when he said, "Which of you with taking thought can add to his stature one cubit? If ye then be not able to do that thing which is least, why take ye thought for the rest?"[16] Jesus just made a nothingness of the subject of thought.

The word of God, that was different: that was quick and powerful, and that "Word was made flesh, and dwelt among us."[17] That Word becomes demonstration; that Word becomes meat, wine, water, and all the rest of these things. The Bible, the tape recordings, and a teacher have a purpose, and that purpose is to bring about a transformation of consciousness from the material sense of existence to the spiritual. The knowledge in and of itself is not power. The knowledge that is in these Infinite Way books or on the tape recordings that we hear, that knowledge is not power. That knowledge is merely the words that we take into our consciousness to help us transform our consciousness until the day comes when consciousness loses much of its material nature.

If we wanted to go on a vacation and needed a hundred dollars for that purpose, and if that is our first thought, that is a degree of material consciousness. If we do not have that as a first thought, however, but our first thought is that the realization of the presence of God makes all things possible, then instead of feeling that we need a hundred dollars, if it is a right activity, the hundred dollars will be there for us to make the trip. The difference is that one person believes that the trip is based on having a hundred dollars, while the other knows that the trip can be provided for by the grace of God and that the hundred dollars is only incidental, the added thing.

The Infinite Invisible
Is the Substance of Life

When we have a materialistic view of life, we are not in the fourth dimension living out from spiritual consciousness. But when it begins to be apparent to us that the silent invisible is actually the substance of our outer living, that is when we are attaining spiritual consciousness. When we think that some material thing is necessary in our experience, that is the material sense of life. When we begin to see that the infinite invisible, the realization of the Christ, the presence of God, is actually the substance of our outer life, then we are in spiritual awareness, and that does not change the fact that the hundred dollars is going to be there just the same. But it was not the hundred dollars that was necessary: it was the realization of God. Sometimes we find that the hundred dollars was not necessary, and that the trip could be made without any money.

The point is that while we are thinking in terms of material form as necessary, we are still in the material sense of life. When we begin to see that the spiritual infinite invisible is the substance of our outer experience, we are then in a spiritual sense of life. That is necessary. Infinite Way writings, the right understanding of scripture and spiritual teaching all play a part in the development of spiritual consciousness.

In proportion then as consciousness is spiritualized, we are able to witness the risen Christ, to witness the ascension, and to witness the sick rise out of their beds, the lame walk, and the blind see. Only in proportion as we see the silent, secret, sacred invisible as the substance of form, the substance of health, the substance of wealth, the substance of all good are we able to let it flow from within, instead of trying to add it to ourselves from without.

Chapter Ten

The Invisible Meat
Unknown to the World

Spiritual living is a complete reversal of material living. We want to cling to our material way of living and have the Spirit add a little more matter to it. It cannot be done. This is one reason that healings do not always take place or do not take place as rapidly as they might or should. We turn to the Spirit and want It to produce matter.

Spiritual living is based on the principle that truth, good, substance, law, life, and supply are within ourselves. This is the foundation of all spiritual living. As sons of God, we are equal heirs to all the heavenly riches; but these riches are always within us, for the kingdom of God is within.

No Wants, Desires, or Needs in Spiritual Living

If we want to live spiritually, we can no longer live from the material basis of wanting, desiring, or needing. We have to begin to reverse that by knowing the truth:

"I and my Father are one,"
1 and all that the Father has is mine.
Because I and the Father are one,

I am infinite, heir of God,
and I can share the allness of the Father.
I drop my burdens at His feet.

But what do we do if we declare that in one breath, and then believe that we are dependent on parents, husband, children, or the government? Is it not clear why some persons defeat their own demonstration? They declare in one breath the spiritual nature of their being, and in the next breath say, "Lend me"; "Give me"; "I earned this from you; I deserve this from you"; or "You are my relative, so you owe it to me." It is right for us to share with one another; it is right for husbands to share with their wives, and wives to share with their husbands, but because it is right does not mean that spiritually the sharing with, or dependence on, someone close to us is necessary. It is not.

Sharing but Not Dependency

From a spiritual standpoint we have to take the attitude that since we are one with the Father our supply is not dependent on human relationships. When we demonstrate that, we can share as generously as we like, and others can share with us as generously as they like. The sin would be if we said they owed it to us, "Look what I have done for you; I deserve it." That is a spiritual sin; that is missing the mark of perfection.

For example, I am in this work, but I am not in this work for your sake. I am in this work because the grace of God pushed me into it to reveal God's grace and God's law on earth. If others are led to come and partake of it, that is their good fortune, and it shows that they are receiving God's grace. But I am not doing this for their sake. I am doing this only because the work of revealing spiritual principles on earth has been given me. To whom they are revealed is not my affair, nor is who comes to partake of it any of my business. Therefore, I have no right to say to a person, "You owe me anything." No, no one owes me anything.

In our family life, we all are happy to share, but how sad it is if members of our family make us feel that we owe it to them. That does something to us.

Nothing could be more satisfying in the world than for each one of us to help support our government willingly and joyously. But when the representatives of the government come with their heavy voices and say, "You are holding it back. Come on, give up! You have a nickel there that you did not declare," that brings out resentment and anger. Then we feel, "It is no joy to support our government; it has become a burden." It should not be that way, and it would not be that way if it were put in the right light.

Dying to a Materialistic Way of Life

We cannot hold onto our materialistic thought and make very rapid progress in a spiritual teaching. We must yield, make an about-face, and actually declare to ourselves that we are spiritual and that we live by God's grace, and then begin to open out a way for that splendor imprisoned within to escape. I like to think of it as tithing with God, or giving the first fruits to God. This applies, not only to money, but to every phase of our lives.

As we know, praying for our friends avails nothing. But in giving the first fruits to God, we must have some period of the day set aside for praying for the enemy, for forgiving our enemy, forgiving seventy times seven until we come to that place where we can truthfully say, "I have naught against any man, even those that I see doing wrong. Forgive them Father, I understand why they are doing it: they do not know their relationship to You; they know nothing about living by Grace and so they have to live by might and by power, any way they can."

Those who come to a spiritual teaching must learn that the major part of this work is dying daily, that is, being transformed through the renewing of the mind, or being renewed through

the transforming of the mind, dying to that sense of material-
ism that desires and seeks to get. As is implied in one of the
Wisdoms of *The Infinite Way*, the greatest of all sins is desire,
because the desire for anything is an acknowledgment of lack.
But if we are one with the Father, how can there be a lack?

If we want to live spiritually, we must acknowledge that we
have. To such a statement the response may be, "Ah, but I do
not have the rent." We are not talking about matter; we have left
that part out. We are not talking about an automobile that we
do not have, nor are we going to God for an automobile or for
money. We are going to God for spiritual wisdom, spiritual
enlightenment, spiritual grace, and that we have. The moment
we allow ourselves to come down to thinking in terms of the
material, we have left the kingdom of God. But the Master said,
"My kingdom is not of this world,"² so the moment we let our
thought come down to "this world," we have left "My kingdom," and we are a "house divided against itself."

It is difficult: of course it is difficult. Even the Master said
that it was not easy. "Strait is the gate, and narrow is the way,
which leadeth unto life, and few there be that find it."³ Why?
Because, like Lot's wife, we begin to leave that old materialistic
state of consciousness and then turn around and miss some of
the things on which we used to spend most of our time to the
detriment of our spiritual progress. In so doing we have lost our
demonstration.

Once we have turned our thought toward the Spirit, we
must keep it on that level. If temporarily it means putting up
with some pain, some economic lack, or some inharmonious
human condition, so be it. We keep our vision on "My kingdom," because it is not possible to have "My kingdom" and "this
world," too.

Traditional metaphysical teaching has had as its object the
turning of bad humanhood into good humanhood, lacking
humanhood into abundant humanhood, sick humanhood into
well humanhood, and if we read the testimonies or listen to

them, we can see that that is what most persons expect. They went to God and got a new automobile; they went to their practitioner and their business doubled, or they went to a practitioner and sold their property. In other words, they were living a double life: half in Spirit, half in matter.

When we come to the spiritual life, we are not thinking in terms of turning lack into abundance, or ill health into good health: we are thinking only in terms of seeking the kingdom of God and His righteousness, and letting the things be added unto us.

The Realization of God Is Fulfillment

Everyone who has attained a touch of the Spirit discovers that the activity of the Spirit within goes before to "make the crooked places straight."[4] When Moses was leading the Hebrew people out of Egypt, with the Red Sea before him and Pharaoh's army behind him, he was in a tough spot. I am sure that what Moses did then was to lift up his eyes and say, "Father, here I am, and here You are. You have just revealed to me that 'I Am That I Am,'[5] which means that where I am You are, for we are one; where You are, I am. This very place whereon I stand is holy ground, and You are here."

In the realized presence of God, Moses found fulfillment: the waters receded, and he and his people walked across on dry land. Did he think about making a demonstration of dry land or a demonstration of rolling back the Red Sea? No, he made a demonstration of realizing the presence of God. When his people were out in the wilderness and had no food, can we imagine that he prayed to God to send them food? He had already learned the nature of God:

> God is spirit; God is I; God is invisible; God is
> omnipresence; God is where I am. Therefore,
> God is my bread, and I have hidden manna.

In that realization, manna fell from the sky. Let us never think that Moses dreamed about manna or water coming from the rocks. All he knew was the presence of God.

Spiritually, we cannot demonstrate supply. Spiritually, we cannot demonstrate health. Spiritually, we cannot demonstrate transportation or parking places. The only thing we can demonstrate is the presence of God, omnipresent here and now, as the very *I* that we are.

> *I* in the midst of me is mighty.
> *I* in the midst of me is a stronghold.
> *I* will never leave me nor forsake me.
> *I* am the bread, the wine, and the water.

> My supply will never forsake me,
> for *I* is my supply. I carry it with me,
> and now I have opened out a way for it
> to escape and appear as manna,
> ravens bringing food, the widow sharing,
> or in countless other ways.

Nonattachment to the Things of "This World"

To embark on the spiritual path means to give up the desire for a better "this world" or for more of "this world", and ask ourselves, "What is *My* kingdom? What did the Master mean when he said, 'My peace I give unto you: not as the world giveth'?"[6] Was he not indicating that there is a peace that more dollars, more manna, or more housing cannot give? Do we not all know people with beautiful homes, cars, and yachts who have not yet found peace, harmony, safety, or security? If anyone could find those things with money or matter, then all the wealthy people would have peace, harmony, safety, and security, and all the poor would not. We know better than that. It is not the having or not having the things of "this world" that makes for peace, contentment, and harmony. It is having *My* grace, because when we have *My* grace, the realization of *My* presence, we have everything needful and twelve basketsful left over.

How often do women go to their wardrobes, take a cursory look and say, "I haven't a thing to wear," declaring lack in the midst of abundance. Instead they must make an about-face and realize:

> I have God's grace to wear;
> I have God's grace inside and outside;
> I am clothed with the heavenly robe,
> spiritual garments, and spiritual jewels.
> All this I have by the grace of God.

Such a realization usually results in an abundance of the outer things, but without any sense of attachment to them. No longer is there a feeling that we must have certain things or be miserable. Rather there is the feeling always of wanting to share what we have because we realize its source.

The great barrier to spiritual demonstration is seeking spiritual light and then looking outside for material gain. Instead we are called upon to live, move, and have our being in spiritual realization, and then the things of this outer world take care of themselves.

The Revelation of God as I

Spiritual living is based entirely on the realization of God as *I*. When Moses had his revelation, the name of God was given to him, but because the Hebrews had not had the opportunity for spiritual enlightenment he knew that if he were to say to them, "*I* am God," they would worship him. If he said, "You are God," they would go out and act as if they were. So the true name of God was hidden from the Hebrew people.

Only the high priests were allowed to know that secret name of God. Furthermore, they were only allowed to voice it at certain times of the year when they were in the inner sanctuary, in the holy of holies, where no one else could hear. Then they could voice the *I*. So from the time of Moses until the time of Jesus, the name *I Am* remained hidden. One of the few Hebrew sects that knew this secret, however, was the Essenes, which was the order in which Jesus was taught, and from which he graduated to become a Hebrew rabbi.

Knowing this secret, he broke the tradition of centuries and began to teach the people: *I* am the way, the truth and the life; *I* am the resurrection; *I* am the bread, the meat, the wine, and the water. Although his disciples and apostles understood this, and some of his other followers also, after the work was organized, many went back to believing that only the *I* of Jesus was the spiritual source. So they set up a worship of one individual, whereas the whole message of Jesus was that we are of one household, and for each of us the Father is the *I* within.

When Jesus fed the multitudes and they followed him across the lake and wanted to be fed the next day, inwardly he must have felt, "Why come to me? I showed you yesterday how the feeding is done by the name of God, *I*. *I* and my Father are one, and all that the Father has is mine. After you have learned that lesson, why come back to me to be fed, when you, too, can open out a way for the imprisoned splendor to escape?"

Sharing the Infinity Within

Many people fail to be helped through spiritual means because while looking to the Spirit they are at the same time a house divided against themselves, seeking their good in material ways and thinking that God is just going to help along a little bit. It is not much different from the orthodox believers who pray to God for their health and then hire half a dozen doctors to help God along.

As fast as possible, we must give up resorting to material means, whether it is borrowing money, begging for it, or just expecting that because someone close to us has it that he owes it to us or should give or share it with us. We must die to our materialistic sense as rapidly as possible and lean more and more heavily on the truth that we are joint-heirs with God. Since each one of us has the same inheritance, each of us can look to his source, but this can be only if we have brought God down from heaven and placed Him in the midst of us, realizing that we can open out a way to release the infinity within by beginning to share: share our prayers, share our forgiveness, share our love, share our possessions, share anything; draw out from within; and the greater the lack seems to be, pour out that much more.

Suggestion Fails Because an Immunity Is Built Up

In metaphysics where mental treatments are used, there is another reason for delayed healings and sometimes failure to heal. In the beginning, metaphysical work was on a mental plane; none of it was spiritual. It is sad to think that in the early days words like "God" and "Christ" were used in their litera-ture, when what those metaphysicians were talking about was their own mind and thoughts. They honestly believed that their mind was God and that thought was power. That error of floun-dering around, believing that the mind was God and that thought is power cost the world seventy-five years of spiritual unfoldment.

In those days, even though the words "God," "Christ," "Spirit," and "prayer," were used, all that was meant was the power of mind over mind and the power of mind over matter. Because up to that time the human mind had never been played on, it was receptive and responsive to suggestion, so that when those early practitioners said to a patient, "You are well and you know it; you are God's perfect child; you are spiritual; you are harmonious; you are well; you are healthy; you are wealthy", the mind of the patient drank in those impressions and suggestions, and he responded. It was a mild form of hypnotism that we can call suggestion.

These early metaphysicians also taught another form of suggestion which is today called "auto-suggestion." They hypnotized themselves by repeating, "I am well; I am spiritual; I am God's perfect child"; and they kept that up until they believed it. This was effective in those early days, because at that time the human mind had not been manipulated by other minds, and it was easy to take an individual and "suggestionize" him, and by repeating those statements and impressing them upon his consciousness, he responded. He got well and had an abundance of this world's goods.

What happened in the following years is that the human mind eventually built up an immunization against mental powers, so that the persons who twenty or thirty years ago could be treated mentally and who responded at that time, today could be treated from now until doomsday and not show the slightest response, because they have built up a complete immunity against suggestion.

Every time we touch a person's thought mentally with suggestion, even though he may respond that time, we are helping him develop an immunity which will prevent him from responding the next time. If it is kept up long enough, he will develop a perfect immunity, and he will never be able to be healed mentally. That is the main reason that some metaphysical movements are smaller today than they were thirty years ago: lack of healings. If healings were taking place on the mental level the way they did thirty or forty years ago, the metaphysical movement would be booming all over the world. It prospers where there are a few individuals who in one way or another have risen higher than the teaching they are voicing, because mental treatment, whether in metaphysics, in psychology, or psychiatry, must fail.

Spiritual Treatment Is Always Given to Ourselves

If the same thing should become true in a spiritual activity and healings did not take place and people did not have improved lives as a result of their spiritual study, it, too, would go by the boards. It is noteworthy, however, that wherever spiritual truth has found its way into a metaphysical movement, even if it is only half the teaching, that teaching continues to flourish. In other words, where there is a small degree of spirituality, it offsets all the mistakes of mentality.

Metaphysically speaking, the world is going through an overturning, and those who have not yet changed from a completely mental treatment basis to a spiritual practice must eventually do so, because the spiritual practice is constantly increasing and is proving itself more effective.

As we know the truth of omnipresence, omnipotence, and omniscience, for at least a moment we forget the patient and his claim, and when he telephones us, he tells us about a healing or improvement, not because we forgot him, but because we remembered omnipresence. We do not give a treatment to a person: we give a treatment to ourselves, and not about the claim. We let the treatment be a realization and a declaration of God, Spirit, and then we do not look around for matter, not even for improved matter. Instead we keep our vision on the truth that "My kingdom is not of this world."[7] If we seek only "My kingdom," the things will be added unto us.

Judge Not According to the Appearance

The work is always to keep our mind stayed on God, and not divide it between God and taking the temperature or looking to see if the lump is coming down. We keep consciousness imbued with truth: the truth of spirit, spiritual law, spiritual life, spiritual immortality—not longevity. If we hope to make somebody live a dozen more years, he will finally reach eighty or ninety anyway, and we may give up in disgust and say, "Now what can I do about it? He is too old to live."

Nobody is too old to live, and nobody is too old to live joyously and harmoniously if he can catch the vision of God as life—not as a person's life being prolonged, made healthier or wealthier, but God as the life of individual being. Life, then, must be infinite in every form of manifestation. We cannot be a house divided against ourselves, but steadfastly we must keep our vision on spiritual truth and spiritual demonstration. The only demonstration we want is the demonstration of God's grace, and that we bring about, not by declaring a lack of it, but by declaring its presence, even in spite of evidence to the contrary.

"Judge not according to the appearance, but judge righteous judgment."[8] Just because the pocketbook seems empty, we do not say, "I do not have," because at the time the only thing we do not have is money. Actually we have that same spirit of God in us, whether we have a great deal of money or a little money. Paul declared that he had as much of God's care when he was dead as when he was alive. "Neither death, nor life. . . shall be able to separate us from the love of God"[9]—neither life nor death! Even "though I walk through the valley of the shadow of death, I will fear no evil: for thou art with me.[10]. . . If I make my bed in hell, behold, thou art there,"[11] but not by declaring, "God, why hast Thou forsaken me," not by declaring, "I do not have enough supply today, I wonder where God is," or "The pain still continues; where is God?" That is a house divided against itself.

We must live, move, and have our being in the realization of spiritual omnipresence, and we must look for spiritual grace, for spiritual harmony, spiritual health, spiritual abundance, and be single-minded. When we do that, the manna falls day by day. As a need appears, fulfillment appears. If we continue to live in the kingdom of God, eventually abundance flows and overflows. That is the nature of God.

The only reason we are not demonstrating it more fully is that degree in which we are a house divided against itself, in which we are talking about Spirit and then looking to see what make of automobile we have to prove how spiritual we are or how many dollars we have as evidence of how spiritual we are. It has nothing to do with how many dollars we have, what make automobile we have, or how big our home is. All that we need is the realization of spiritual grace and spiritual harmony, and as we dwell "in the secret place of the most High"[12] and our thought is far removed from material concerns, then we find abundance flowing and overflowing, and of course it is because our desire has not been for those things.

Replace Desire With Fulfillment

According to *The Infinite Way,* one of the greatest sins is desire. Desire must be replaced with the realization of the fullness of life lived in God's presence. Therefore, our entire seeking must be for God's presence for in that presence is fullness of joy, infinite abundance, pressed down and running over. Few experience this because what most of us desire is to keep what we have, and have a little more of it.

It should be a bit easier for us to make that jump if we stop to realize that when we leave this particular plane we check everything at the probate court. We have to enter the next plane without money, without clothing, and without housing. It must be a strange place. The only thing that seems to have been retained from this world is a music department for harps and a costume department for robes, but otherwise heaven apparently is devoid of all these material wonders. I never heard of a Cadillac in heaven.

So, when we stop to realize that we live beyond the grave, and live free of all ugly encumbrances, it should be easy for us eventually to take that next step and enter "My kingdom" without a thought for what we shall eat or what we shall drink, or wherewithal we shall be clothed, not one single thought about any material encumbrance. We go right up into that heavenly realm, a pure state of consciousness.

The True Name

The name of the Father within is *I,* or what Paul called "Christ in you."[13] The Christ in the Hebrew and Aramaic is the Messiah, and in the Oriental teaching is Buddha, so when the Christ is called Messiah It is Jewish, but in Christian terms It is called the Christ, and in Buddhist terminology It is the Buddha, all meaning the same thing: the source of light, enlightenment, savior, enlightened one. The Messiah, the Christ, or the Buddha is the enlightened one. When we understand that, then we understand that the name of Messiah, the Christ, or the Buddha is *I.* That is the true name that was hidden from the world from the beginning: *I.* That was what was revealed to Moses when he was on the highest mountain of spiritual illumination. It was revealed to him: "I Am That I Am."

Every Oriental mystic has had that same revelation. There is only one ego, and the name is *I.* It makes no difference where we search in mysticism, the name and nature of God is *I.*

Mystics have been hesitant to reveal this to the masses, because someone is likely to come along, organize it, and then make them believe and say, "I am God." No human being is God, and not only that, no human being has the right to say, "I am God." But every spiritual student who meditates will one day hear the voice say, "Know ye not that *I* am God?" Then, if he is wise, and people seek him out for teaching, eventually he can reveal to them that *I* in the midst of them is God. The kingdom of God is within us, and that *I* in the midst of us is the bread, meat, wine, and water. *I* in the midst of us is the power of resurrection.

Many of us, who have been in the healing work have had occasion to work with patients who were near death's door and were called incurable, have had the experience in meditation of hearing the voice say, "This is my beloved Son, in whom I am well pleased."[14] Yet if we opened our eyes and looked at them we would not think so, but here it was being revealed spiritually, "This is my beloved Son, in whom I am well pleased." When the voice spoke that way, harmony came; the patient was restored, because in truth whether we are living or dying, God is in the midst of us. Whether we are alive or dead, we still have God's presence and God's care, God's support, God's allness. But to bring it into manifestation, we must say as did Paul, "Neither death, nor life. . . shall be able to separate us from the love of God," for the name of God is *I*.

If we destroy this temple, *I* in the midst of us will raise it up again. *"I Am That I Am";* but never let a human being claim that about his humanhood. We do not repeat it to anyone, but when someone has come to us sacredly for spiritual instruction and we feel he is ready for the revelation, then we can reveal to him the wisdom of the ages: there is no God separate and apart from us. God is manifested as us. Our very consciousness is the temple of God; even our body is the temple of God. "The place whereon thou standest is holy ground,"[15] for God embodies our supply. We could live for five hundred years and never want, for the *I* in the midst of us has the fullness of all that we will ever need unto the end of the world, unto the end of any need for any earthly thing.

We seek not the earthly things, but seek the realization of the presence of God within, and then without our taking thought, all these things will be added to us, because this presence within us knows that we have need of these things, and it is Its good pleasure to give us the kingdom, if only we can rest in this Word.

I in the midst of you am mighty.
I in the midst of you will feed you,
satisfy you, clothe you, house you, transport you.

I in the midst of you go before you
to prepare mansions for you.
Rest only in My word,
let My word rest in you.

There is an invisible robe, the garment of spirit, and it is upon us. It clothes us; it appears outwardly as whatever clothing we need, but only because of our realization that, unseen to human sight, we are wearing the spiritual robe. We will be fed with food in the outer without taking thought, without struggle, but first we must remember, I have "hidden manna.[16]. . . I have meat to eat that ye know not of."[17]

To find our freedom from any sense of lack and limitation, we must never forget this passage:

"I have meat to eat that ye know not of."
I have within my own consciousness,
within my own soul,
spiritual garments, spiritual housing,
spiritual transportation, omnipresence Itself.
I have meat that the physical eye
cannot see, and by abiding in that,
the outer food is always there.

As we rest in that invisible meat within, life is lived without concern for the future or the past, but in the grace of this moment of I Am–ness. This is the mystical life.

TAPE RECORDED EXCERPTS
Prepared by the Editor

Communion is an experience which comes to us as the fruitage of a listening attitude when a depth of inner silence is experienced, as the following excerpts indicate.

Communion

"Our prayer is the ability to commune within ourselves with the transcendental presence which we know is the very soul of our being. It is closer to us than breathing, and therefore, we can commune with It in silence. Communion is a silence, because it is not necessary for words to pass from us to God. God is already the all-knowing. In our attitude of listening, we are receptive and responsive to the presence and the power of God, to the will of God, to the way of God, to the thoughts of God.

"Sometimes the still small voice does speak; sometimes It thunders, but always when It speaks, the earth melts. For It to speak does not necessarily mean using language, for God can speak to us also in just an inner warmth, a glow, a feeling of the presence, an awareness of something greater than human expression, and that, of course, is the divine communion."

Joel S. Goldsmith, "God as the Soul of Man and the Universe," *The 1963 Instructions for Teaching the Infinite Way.*

"You can talk about God, and you can think about God, . . . but that does not bring God into your experience. . . . God comes into your experience in a moment of silence, . . . in a moment that ye think not, and in that moment the bridegroom cometh. In that one second when the human mind is still, the experience of God comes. . . . The practice of meditation leads us to that point where the mind can be still. . . . It is when we get through with talking, thinking, or reading that the experience comes, and then you will understand what it means to live not by law but by Grace."

Joel S. Goldsmith, "Grace, the Purpose of Meditation," *"The 1959 Hawaiian Village Open Class.*

"Meditation is really the gateway to heaven, if meditation is understood. . . . You cannot be at peace if you want something. You cannot be at peace if you have a desire. You cannot be at peace if you are longing for something, or if you are feeling a sense of separation. You can only be at peace when you are in communion with the divine spirit. . . .

"With practice, we do get to that place where, if someone asks for help, we sit in that silence contemplating God's presence, making no attempt to heal anyone, save anyone, redeem anyone, reform anyone, or even forgive anyone. Now we are in the realization of God alone: Thy grace is my sufficiency, and his and hers. And with this first success comes a measure of healing. It takes a great deal of practice. It takes weeks and months, and it takes a lot of sins and diseases rendered null and void before we actually come to a place where it is automatic to sit down and rejoice in God's presence, without wanting God to do something for us."

Joel S. Goldsmith, "The Way of Meditation,"
The 1959 Hawaiian Village Open Class.

Chapter Eleven

Infinite Uncircumscribed
Being

Most persons, regardless of their religious background, have the idea that God's grace, God's blessing, or the giving-ness of God is dependent on some thing. Often it has been taught that the receiving of God's benefits is dependent on our obedience to the Ten Commandments or to church rules, regular attendance in church, taking communion, fasting, sacrificing, tithing, being grateful, or having faith.

Releasing God

An important part of our work is releasing God in the sense of realizing that we do not need God for anything except for God to be God, which God always is. We stop looking to God to do something for us now or in the future, since whatever God does, God has been doing from everlasting to everlasting. God never changes. God never inaugurates something now; He could not heal us now; He could not heal us tomorrow.

We come to this awareness through the progressive unfold-ment of Infinite Way principles. First, must come the realization that God is not a withholding God; therefore, if God is not a withholding God, God cannot be a giving God, because giving something now would imply having withheld it up to now. In God there is no such thing as giving or withholding: there is only God being God. But God is being God eternally; God has been God eternally. Our function is not to reach out to God as if we wanted something of God, but rather to tune in to God as if we had been disconnected, and as if we are now reconnecting ourselves with God.

Then, another step to help us gain this awareness is to see that God is responsible for the rising and the setting of the sun, and that these are not dependent on anything that man does or does not do. God is responsible for the laws of nature, which are constantly in operation, whether or not man does anything to deserve or be worthy of them. What God is, God is, regardless of man.

God's rain falls "on the just and the unjust,"[1] and there is no such thing as God's blessings being withheld for any reason, and certainly not because of anything we do or do not do. Does this not make it clear that an absence of God's grace has nothing to do with God? It has to do with our violation of some spiritual law or our acceptance of a sense of separation from God, but never in any way because of God.

It takes a while to believe and to be able to come into the consciousness that can accept the truth that the grace of God is not dependent on anything that man does or does not do, but that man's demonstration of God's grace is dependent on his coming into consciousness oneness or at-one-ment with God.

Supply Is Infinite

If we are not demonstrating supply, it is not because we do not attend the right church or were not baptized or confirmed. The world is still full of supply, whether or not we have done these things. The answer lies in the fact that we have not known the truth.

What Have We In Our House?

When we first learn the truth that the demonstration of supply always begins with one passage of scripture, we are better able to understand our failure to demonstrate supply: "What hast thou in the house?"² What have we in our house? We should have realized ages ago that since God is infinite and since the promise is, "Son, . . . all that I have is thine,"³ and God has given man dominion, it must necessarily follow that man has dominion over supply and that he has an infinity of supply.

So the demonstration of supply is dependent, not on how much we receive, but on how much we give out, because our storehouse is already full. God is individual consciousness; God is the source of supply; therefore, individual consciousness is the source of supply. It is not barren; it is not an empty storehouse. Since God constitutes individual consciousness, individual being is as infinite in substance and supply as is God.

When we accept the truth that "I and my Father are one,"⁴ not two, we realize that in this oneness we have an infinity of supply. To demonstrate that, if we have a few drops of oil and a little meat, we have to begin giving it, pouring it, sharing it at every level of life, giving the first fruits to God. The giving and sharing of material possessions is, however, one of the easiest of demonstrations. But since God is spirit, the major part of our demonstration is really at the spiritual level, and that embraces going within ourselves and forgiving, sharing, serving, surrendering, giving up those qualities that act as a barrier to the divine, recognizing the spiritual nature of all mankind, and in every possible way pouring it out from ourselves.

The Omnipresence of Supply

Those who understand this principle of giving never know lack or limitation. In a circumstance such as Moses encountered with the Hebrew people, where there could not conceivably be a sufficient supply of food or drink, he brought it forth in what seemed to be miraculous ways. Even when the Master was in the wilderness, where apparently there was not an abundance, it was brought forth, in what appeared as a miracle. It would be impossible to be any place where supply is not, because it would be impossible to be any place where God is not.

The demonstration of supply is based on one truth: God, or spirit, is supply. God is the bread, the meat, the wine, and the water, so how much bread, meat, wine, and water do we have? God is the fortress and the high tower, so how much protection and safety and security do we have?

In our materialistic sense of life, we believe that a bomb-proof shelter is security and that money is supply, thereby cutting ourselves off from the infinity of supply that is already at hand and which will manifest itself in the necessary forms. When we believe that supply consists in some of its manifested forms, such as coal, oil, gold, silver, diamonds, bread, or meat, we cut ourselves off from supply, but that does not mean that there is any lack of supply. It is still infinite, and it is still omnipresent.

What does omnipresence mean? Does it not imply the omnipresence of God, the omnipresence of spirit, the omnipresence of allness, the omnipresence of life, truth, love, and substance, and therefore, the omnipresence of supply? But we acknowledge omnipresence in one breath and deny it in the next.

The secret of supply is to acknowledge omnipresence, since in our oneness with the Father there is the omnipresence of spirit, and spirit is the substance of all form. Having the substance of all form, the form must appear. To prove this is not to look about to receive it; that is what cuts us off from it. It is in seeking out ways to express it.

Releasing Supply

We may come to the end of our rope and believe we have nothing left, but that cannot be true, because omnipresence is still there. The presence of the bread of life is still there, the wine, and the water, so no matter how barren we seem to become, we are still filled. It means that we have to search deeper until we find in our house that which we are keeping dammed up.

If we learn this lesson and begin on some particular day to set aside a certain percentage of everything that comes in and give the first fruits to God, then after our obligations are met, we can share the rest with our neighbor in accordance with the love-thy-neighbor-as-thyself principle. We search around to discover what measure of unforgiveness is locked up in us and weed it out until that part is completed. We seek to render some service that we either owe to another or if we do not owe it, feel that it would be loving to share it. We continue searching within our consciousness as long as there appears to be a lack, because the only lack is in drawing it up out of our consciousness. The lack is not external to us.

When we have learned that lesson and put it into practice, and the abundance begins to flow, we see clearly that it never had been withheld because of God, but because of our ignorance of truth. God was not withholding it, and it did not come to us because we did something to earn it, deserve it, or be worthy of it. All we did was come into the awareness of the truth that we already have in the house.

Truth Makes Free

The same thing is true in the healing of any situation of human experience: physical, mental, moral, financial, political, or relationships. Whatever the healing may be, it is not because God suddenly deigns to do something, nor is it because we have contacted God. It has to do with the fact that we have discovered the truth, and it is the truth that makes us free.

Very often when there is a lack of healing, the reason for such lack is an undiscovered truth. In the case of those who are not very far along on the path, the greater responsibility lies with the practitioner. But with those who have gone some distance on the path, there is a responsibility for them to look within and see if they are fulfilling the teaching by which they are supposed to be living. They cannot go on forever benefitting by the grace of the practitioner's consciousness and ignoring their own responsibility to live the spiritual life.

It is difficult to come to that place where we understand that it is not something we have done or left undone that releases God's good in our experience. That has not influenced God to withhold anything from us: it is a barrier we have erected by not knowing the truth.

God is the same always, but the miracle is that God is omnipresent, that there is no way to get outside the realm of God, although we can shut ourselves off from realizing God's grace by sin or by ignorance of truth. God does not shut Himself off from us: we shut ourselves off from God, and that is the big lesson to be learned. The availability of God is always the same, even in hell, even in "the valley of the shadow of death."[5] It takes an act of awareness on our part: "Ye shall know the truth, and the truth shall make you free."[6] So it is that, as we know the truth about supply and begin to fulfill the laws of supply, we have an abundance of it. As we begin to understand the laws of health and fulfill those laws, we have an abundance of health. Why? Nobody is withholding it from us but ourselves, and the knowing of the truth sets us free.

Do Not Be Satisfied
Merely With Human Good

Humanly, we are trained to rest in, and to be satisfied with, human harmony. We are completely at rest when we have sense of health. A body may be diseased, but as long as we do not know it and as long as it is not paining us, we are usually at peace. So, too, a person who has a position with a fairly good income is accustomed to feeling at peace. The fact that unemployment may be right around the corner, for one reason or another, is not disturbing him at the moment, because at this moment everything outwardly appears to be alright. Over the centuries we have developed a nature that makes it possible for us to feel at peace, as long as the body is not paining and the pocketbook not straining.

However, when we come to a spiritual teaching, there is a need to make a transition in consciousness to where we realize that neither supply nor health is in the body, the pocketbook, or the bank account. Both of these are activities of consciousness and must be found in consciousness. There is a spiritual source of health and supply which we have to contact.

So it is that a dangerous place for every person on this path is the place where things are going along beautifully. Things may be going beautifully as a result of the practitioner's work, but he may have brought the patient only up to the sense of physical health or supply, and not helped him make that transition which everyone must make.

Spiritual Harmony,
the Fruitage of a Transition in Consciousness

Our righteousness must exceed that of the Scribes and the Pharisees.[7] How much righteousness is that? They were already perfect human beings. The greater righteousness is where we have realized the truth with which Jesus responded when he was called good. "Why callest thou me good? there is none good but one, that is, God."[8] There is but one health: God is "the health of my countenance."[9] That is quite different from saying, "I am well because my heart beats all right and my lungs breathe all right." Here is a transition from resting in a healthy body to the demonstration of spiritual harmony.

Nobody can describe what this transition involves because it is something that comes to us with the realization that germs are not power, that weather or climate is not power:

> Certainly, the I of me is power;
> the omnipresence of God is power.
> But God is not in the whirlwind;
> therefore, power is not in the whirlwind.
> Power is not out here in germs;
> power is not out here in weather or climate.
> Supply is not out here in dollars or gold mines.
> God is my supply; God is my safety and security.

Something happens inside of us when we realize that physical protection is relatively unimportant. Many persons who have a great deal of physical protection find it does not assure their safety. We are hid with Christ in God. We live, and move, and have our being in God, and that is not an affirmation: that is truth. Although it is truth, it cannot become true in our experience until we have some definite realization of it. We have to have a moment of realization that God alone governs our life and that we are not affected by externals. We need not fear what the mortal scene can do to us. Why? Because I-and-the-Father-are-one is something more than a statement: it has become a realization.

It is for this reason that in our meditations we should always take some specific subject for pondering, for contemplative meditation, to see if eventually we can gain the consciousness of it. We may have to meditate dozens of times on the same subject. So we work with supply, safety, security, or peace in our contemplative meditation until something from within responds and we say, 'Whereas I was blind, now I see,'[10] now I know, now I feel, now I am aware that God is my supply; God is my health."

There is not God and health; God cannot give health. God cannot send health; and God is not the medium by which health is gained. God, Itself, is health. When that becomes a living fire inside, then health is not dependent on the external realm.

So we discover that our good is not dependent on God

doing something: it is dependent on our knowing the truth that God *is* that something. With omnipresence, omnipotence, and omniscience, we have the whole secret which is that our good is an activity of truth consciously realized. When we realize consciously the truth of supply, the truth of health, the truth of relationships, the truth of peace on earth, that is what we demonstrate. It was there always because of omnipresence, but now we know the truth and are consciously aware of it.

Omnipresence Functions Only in the Now

Looking for anything in the future cuts us off from supply, health, or whatever appears to be necessary. Looking to the future is a barrier that separates us from our good, because God cannot exist in the future. God is omnipresence, and that omnipresence is only now. Whatever truth is, truth is truth now. There is no future about it; there is no past about it, because everything exists at the standpoint of *now.*

If there are no coconuts on the trees at this moment, it does not indicate an absence of God; it does not indicate the barrenness of the tree. It indicates the season of rest and, if we could see inside the tree, we would know that God is functioning in the omnipresence of now. As long as we abide in that truth, the coconuts will come forth in due season. Wherever there are peach trees laden with peaches today, or pear trees with pears, or wherever there is watermelon growing, if we could look in on those trees or vines on a midwinter day, they would testify only to barrenness. Then we might say, "Look how absent God is." But omnipresence reveals that the processes of nature are taking place right now. They are not taking place in the future, and if those processes are not taking place now, there will be no fruitage in the future.

It has to be in the *now* that omnipresence is functioning. Therefore, regardless of any sense of barrenness at this particular moment in any direction, we have to be willing to look with our inner eye and behold omnipresence functioning now. As long as omnipresence is functioning *now*, and omnipresence is omnipotence, and omnipotence is omniscience, then in due season everything will appear in accordance with its natural operation.

We judge by appearances, and judging by appearances, we declare the absence of God, spirit, the absence of good, but there is no such thing as an absence of God. There is only omnipresence, and omnipresence is functioning now; but if we do not realize omnipresence, we are going to have no fruitage tomorrow, next week, or next month, because the fruitage of next week, next month, and next year is dependent on our knowing the truth, and the only truth there is, is omnipresence.

In spite of any immediate barrenness, if we want fruit in due season, we must realize omnipresence as of this moment, and omnipresence then may plant a seed; it may operate on a seed that is already planted; or it may send a shoot up above the earth. But nothing is going to happen in the future except by reason of our realization of omnipresence now.

Sowing to the Flesh and to the Spirit Now

The meaning of "Whatsoever a man soweth, that shall he also reap"[11] and the meaning of karma is that the thoughts and deeds that we put in operation at this moment must come back to us. Living as human beings, we cannot escape from the law of sowing and reaping; we cannot escape from karma, because we are creating it. If in this moment, we are sowing to the flesh, that is, if we are declaring the opposite of omnipresence, if we are bemoaning our fate, if we are doing anything in the world except relaxing in omnipresence, omnipotence, and omniscience, all we are doing is sowing a lack for next week, next month, next year, or five years from now, because the lack that we experience in this moment is the lack that is going to come back and plague us in its due season.

If we sow to the Spirit, to Truth, we reap life everlasting, but we have to do our sowing now. If we *now* realize our oneness with the Father and realize that all that the Father has is ours, that spirit is the only life and the only law, we are sowing to the Spirit, to Truth, and our demonstration will be life everlasting, life harmonious and abundant.

We are sowing our crops with every breath we breathe, and that which we are sowing is what comes back and which we later reap. God is not going to do anything in the future, but our realization of the omnipresence of God is the assurance that our good is embodied here and now. All it has to do is to come forth into visibility in a now which we call tomorrow, next month, or next year.

We always come back to the center of our being and realize our oneness with the divine. We bring our life to the central point of this instant. It is in this instant that our relationship with God is established, is operative, is functioning, and is bearing fruit. We always come back to this instant. We must break the habit of living in the past and break the habit of living in the future. Certain plans for the future are necessary, but these are always tentative, because they are always based on the will of God. Our major purpose in life, however, is returning to the center and realizing:

> Here and now, I and the Father are one, and that is
> why here and now, there is omnipresence, the
> omnipresence of infinity,
> the omnipresence of omnipotence.

Breaking the Bonds of Limitation

All mankind lives in a squirrel cage. It is the squirrel cage of their own mind. They do not live outside the confines of that mind; they do not know what is going on in the world; they do not know what is going on in the life of men, of women, or of anything. They live only in the embodiment of their own mind;

and they race around from one thing to another, like a squirrel chasing nuts, and that is where most lives are confined, right inside that squirrel cage, around and around.

If we still feel that we are confined to a squirrel cage, we can break that, because actually no one has a right to be living inside his own mind. It is all right to live inside our soul. Then we are living in the life of everybody on earth, because there is only one soul. When we are living within the confines of that tied-up mind, however, we are living only to the personal sense of self, and we are not living out from the center of our being. We break that by coming back to our own center:

> Here, I and the Father are one, and my oneness
> with God constitutes my oneness with all spiritual
> being and idea, with all of God's children and with
> all of God's ideas. I am not confined to this body;
> I am not confined to this mind:
> I am living the life of infinite being.
> I am not circumscribed within the limitations
> of the cradle to the grave.

What we have to do is remember the parenthesis in eternity, and then try to push those bars back, so we are not so confined in the parenthesis of our personal life. We have to live out from a broader outlook and we bring ourselves to this point, not by becoming more worldly, but by realizing our oneness with God and with all spiritual being, even that which calls itself past, present or future, because we are living as infinite uncircumscribed being. Then, when we are in meditation and we have a listening ear, we can bring ourselves a wealth of truth from the entire world, not just a limited aspect of it.

Our life is lived in infinite consciousness rather than in the forms that consciousness assumes, and we turn within to our consciousness to bring forth harmony, peace, justice, benevolence, truth, and love. Always our work is to bring these forth from within our consciousness, not to look to "man, whose breath is in his nostrils,"[12] nor to look to circumstances or conditions for it, but to learn to live so that every day we turn within to see what joys and glories we are going to bring forth from within our own consciousness. This breaks that pattern of the squirrel cage, because when we turn to our consciousness, we are turning to infinity, and we are bringing forth experiences, some of which have never been recorded by man, and others of which have only been recorded by those who have had the deepest spiritual vision.

If it is true that "man shall not live by bread alone, but by every word that proceedeth out of the mouth of God,"[13] then how necessary it is to turn within several times a day for that bread of life, and gradually find that we are not living the life of a squirrel chasing after nuts anymore.

God is always functioning, and God is always functioning at the standpoint of omnipresence, omnipotence, omniscience, and the remedy for our ills is to turn away from living in the outer realm to living as, through, and by an activity of consciousness, always turning within to that consciousness for the fruits of the Spirit: harmony, peace of all kinds, good in every form. It is an activity of truth in our consciousness rather than some external experience or as some favor from God, which it cannot be, because "God is no respecter of persons."[14] God's grace, falls on the just and the unjust. It is omnipresent, available to us through seeking it in our consciousness, rather than in its manifested forms.

TAPE RECORDED EXCERPTS
Prepared by the Editor

Relationships

"As you study the mission of the great Master, Christ Jesus, you will notice him continuing in prayer. . . going away for forty days to the mountains to pray, to meditate, to maintain his conscious contact with God. . . . Then he says, 'I have meat to eat that ye know not of. . . . I am the bread of life.' In order to be able to say that, he has to pray without ceasing. He has to learn to pray for himself, within himself, to himself, in sacredness and in secrecy. He has to learn how to pray for his enemies. He may not have known how to pray for his enemies any more than you or I know at this moment, but it comes by going away in quietness and saying, 'Father, how do I forgive my enemies seventy times seven? How do I have the capacity to forgive those, to bless those, to pray for those who despitefully use me? Show me how to pray. Show me how to forgive. Show me how to be living in spite of all of these harassments and troubles and woes that these people bring upon me. Show me how to stay in the Spirit so that I may ever have this meat and this water and this wine and this bread.'

"So it is with us. The pressure of the world not only would separate us from each other, it would separate buyers and customers. It would separate store owners and employees. It would separate capital and labor. It would separate man from man, man from wife, and wife from husband, and parent from child.

"The pressure of this world is a sense of separation. 'Divide and conquer' is the way of the world. But in spiritual oneness, in spiritual union, there is strength. In our union with God, not in the union of men and women but in our union with God, is the source, the supply, and the infinite nature of our good.

"Be assured that this is not an easy way. The world has made this sense of separation; the world has made us natural enemies toward each other; the world has made one animal to prey upon another, and the great animal, man, to prey upon all the other animals. The world has come of that, and none of this would be. . . if only we were consciously one with God, if only we were united in each other, with each other: I in you and you in me, and all of us in God. That cannot happen out here. That can happen only as an activity of our consciousness. . . .

"The activity of truth in your consciousness becomes the law unto your experience. Remember that without it you are a victim of material and mental laws, but with the activity of truth in your consciousness, you become master of your fate and captain of your soul. You then have God's dominion in your experience, truth-dominion, the activity of truth in your consciousness."

Joel S. Goldsmith, "Psalms 146 and 147,"
The Second 1953 New York Closed Class.

"If you look at man forever and forever through your eyes, you never will behold that which is there to behold. Man is in fact God made evident through spiritual consciousness. It is the allness of God. Individual man is the allness of God appearing here on earth. Every quality of God is embodied in that which we call man. The infinity, the eternality of God is embodied as the immortality of individual being, that which we call man. All that God is, that which we call man is. All that God has belongs to that which we call man, for I and the Father are one. Isn't it sad that we have this poor vision that obscures from us this wonderful picture of each other as we are here at this moment?. . .

"There is more to man than the eyes can behold. It takes that inner attunement to know it, and you can develop it in this way. Begin to withdraw judgment about the people you know. There are plenty you know that you don't like. That is a natural instinct with everybody on earth. And there are those you do like. But you will be surprised that these people you do not like are nothing like that at all and neither are the people you like. They are entirely different. Both of these categories have a something you have not yet discerned, and that is. . . their spiritual being; that is their spiritual inner true selfhood. That is what enabled the Master to discern these qualities in the Magdalene, in the woman taken in adultery, in the thief on the cross. He was not judging by appearances; he was not judging by their exterior: he had discerned in them that which was worthy of redemption. He beheld the Christ of their being, and for them there was no punishment, no waiting, to get into heaven. 'Today shalt thou be with me in paradise.' What? A thief on the cross? No, that was not what he took into paradise. He took the realization of that man's true being. . . .

"Begin with the erroneous side of life and later develop it on the good side of life, to withhold, to withdraw judgment. Do not label anything or anybody good or bad. Do not label anything material or spiritual. Do not label anything sick or well. . . . It is a wonderful thing to find that people whom you have always known all of a sudden are much finer than you ever dreamed, much more wonderful, and they have qualities of a nature you never knew. Why? They are *My* qualities, *My* integrity, not human integrity."

Joel S. Goldsmith, "The Christ,"
The Second 1953 New York Closed Class.

Chapter Twelve

Preparation for the Advent

There is only one God. There is no Hebrew God, Christian God, or Oriental God; there is no God but One. It makes no difference whether that One is worshiped in a Hebrew synagogue, a Christian church, a Mohammedan mosque, or a Buddhist temple; it is still the one God. Even though different persons may follow different paths, all paths lead to one place for there is only one God. Those who truly seek God will find Him, and when they do, they will discover that that God is within their own being.

You, yourself, are the temple of God. Every individual is a temple of God, and God dwells within, that is, the spirit of God dwells within every individual, awaiting his awakening. No person has the capacity to awaken himself; no one of himself has the capacity to seek God. The moment an individual knows that he is seeking God, however, it means that God has already reached him, because the human being, as such, is like a branch of a tree that is cut off from its source. It has no knowledge of its source, and it could not even seek its source. So, when an individual begins to seek its source, it is because the source has already found the individual and has already begun the process of awakening. He may think he is seeking God, forgetting that scripture says, "Ye have not chosen me, but I have chosen you."[1]

States of Consciousness

There are three states of consciousness, and every person goes through all three states and stages before he comes into the realization of the final one: the attainment of union with God, real conscious re-union with God. The cave man represents the first state of consciousness, the animal man, but even in that animal man there is something of the mental stage.

In that cave man or animal state of consciousness, there is also the spiritual, but it is completely hidden. It has not revealed itself to him. It was always there because God is the underlying, animating, causative principle of all there is. There could be no creation of any nature if there were not God. There is no such thing as matter creating itself, so even though a person may look out at a material universe and see nothing but mountains, valleys, rivers, lakes, and oceans, and believe that this is a material universe, once he comes to a place of perception he will know that none of this could exist if there were not an invisible cause. Later he comes to realize that that cause is spiritual.

As man progresses from the caveman state and comes up to a higher degree of civilization, a better mode of life, he becomes less physical and more mental. There is less of the purely animal man, less of the purely physical, a little more of intuition and judgment. He is guided more by the mental than the physical. Eventually he gets to the place where his body, even the universe, is but an instrument for him, and he is himself a mental individual living through a body and in a physical universe.

Up to this point, a person could almost believe there is no God. There is no sign of one, and so far there has been no need for one. Instinct leads the animal to food, clothing, and shelter; instinct leads him to his mate and to everything necessary for human existence. There is no knowledge of God, no awareness of God, and yet behind this whole scene there is God. God is the creator of all that is.

The Search Begins

In the pagan state of life, man is living on both the mental and physical levels of life, but with no knowledge of the spiritual. On this level, man begins to find problems beyond his physical ability to solve and eventually beyond his mental capacities. You can assume that the crops, which had been abundant, do not seem to grow so well. The sea, which had always been full of fish, is beginning to be depleted of fish. The climate, which had seemed to be moderate, now begins to have devastating storms and droughts. There are problems now for which man has no answer. Eventually through these problems he begins to search for something greater than himself.

Can you see what is happening in man's consciousness? For the first time he begins to doubt his self-sufficiency and becomes aware of his inability to solve his own problems, and realizes that there are things in this world greater than his capacity to handle. You can imagine that the struggle is a hard one, because man has awakened sufficiently to be uncomfortable when things are out of control and when there are situations for which he has no answer. It is only after a long, hard struggle that he acknowledges there must be something beyond him, something beyond any man.

When man reaches that stage, he begins searching for that which is above man, greater than man, beyond man, seeking for that which can solve man's unsolvable problems. This led, in pagan days, to the worship of false deities. He may have found a god to worship and to which to pray and sacrifice. He may have believed that he received help from that false god, so he continued to seek that help until probably there was no longer any response, and he searched for, and eventually found, another god; or perhaps he found that his first god would only meet certain problems, and he had to have another god for other problems. Eventually, there was built up a host of gods, and a person could go to one god for one thing, to another god for something else, and to still others gods for other things.

How Forms of Worship Evolved

Man, not recognizing the fact that he was worshiping false gods, began to believe that there was something wrong with his form of worship. Heretofore, he may have been asking God only for things, pleading with God, and begging Him to give him things; but now he became convinced that because God was not answering his pleading he must begin to sacrifice to this God and give up something of value to placate him. In that attempt, there was not only animal sacrifice, but actually human sacrifice, mentioned in the Old Testament as well as in pagan literature.

People began to believe that God is a withholding God, a God that has it in His capacity to give these blessings, but is not doing so; therefore, a way must be found to get God to give those who worshiped Him the blessings they wanted. Through such problems different forms of worship developed, prayer came into existence, sacrifice, holy days, feast days, fast days. All kinds of ways were invented by man in an attempt to force God to give man what he wanted. So all of the various forms of worship that existed in pagan days and all of those that still exist, grew out of man's ignorance of God and out of man's effort to find a way to get God to give him those blessings that he needed but which God seemed to be withholding.

Eventually, as must always be the case, an individual came along who realized this could not be the way or it would be more successful. It was not proving itself; it was not demonstrating itself, so something must be wrong with it. Regardless of how it happened, what did happen was that Abraham established the principle of one God, just One, replacing all those other gods, and it was from this one God that man was to receive all blessings.

The forms of worshiping that one God were, if anything, more nonsensical than are our ways today, and our ways of worship today are nonsensical enough, once the nature of God is perceived. But in those days it was worse. At one time God was even encased in a caravan that went with the Hebrews wherever they went. There was the belief that God was out there in the ark and if that ark were lost in battle, the war would be lost, because if they did not have God, they could not win; and if they lost the ark in which God was confined, they certainly could not win. So the ark became a holy thing in which God was embodied.

Later on this same superstition was given to man in another form, where he was led to believe that God was in church, and therefore, if he went to church he could find God; if he did not go to church, he was not where God was, and so he was godless.

That first turning to something greater than himself, however, marks the most important step in the unfoldment of man's consciousness, because no matter how many false steps a person takes, there is at least the conviction that the solution to problems lies in something higher than human wisdom or human strength.

God Has Chosen You

While you may be led up many blind alleys, as long as you persist, as long as you do not become discouraged by your failures, you will eventually come to the kingdom of God which is within yourself. When you are no longer easily discouraged in your search for God and if you have reached a place where you realize that your form of worship has not brought forth the demonstration of harmony but nevertheless you still persist, it really means that the spirit of God has touched you, and that It is trying to lead you back to Itself.

No matter how many false turns you take, no matter how many false starts you make, no matter how many failures you have, remember that these are all due to your ignorance of the nature of God. These failures will continue, but the fact that you continue on the path, letting nothing turn you away, even if God has not answered your prayers today, is the proof that the spirit of God has touched you, and that It will not let you rest until It catches up with you, and until you abide in stillness and let the realization of its presence dawn in your consciousness.

All those on the spiritual path are companions and friends, each helping the other. One person catches a bit of light a little sooner than another, is a step ahead, and becomes a light for others along the way. Another one catches a glimpse of God and becomes the bridge over which others travel to reach that haven, revealing what he has discovered.

Your persistence on the spiritual path means that the spirit of God has already touched you. You have not chosen God. God has chosen you, and God will not let you go until you arrive safely at home in His bosom. The constant recognition that the spirit of God has touched you and will not let you go is one of the greatest helps on the way.

The Preparation for the Spiritual Experience

God cannot reveal Himself to you except in proportion to your preparedness to receive Him. One of the most important words in your vocabulary at this part of your search is the word *preparation,* preparation for the advent of the birth of the Christ within. There must be a preparation. How clearly this is brought out in the story of the immaculate conception! Why was Mary chosen to receive the conception and birth of the Christ? She was a virgin, obedient, and humble. Had she not been that, she would not have been prepared for the experience.

If you examine the life of every spiritual leader, you will find that in one way or another there was a preparation for the experience, and I am not referring to being merely humanly good. Being humanly good may not necessarily be a preparation for the spiritual experience. As a matter of fact, some well-known religious leaders were anything but humanly good, nevertheless they were overtaken by the spirit of God. Paul, as a persecutor and killer of Christians, could hardly have been said to be humanly good. There are so many who may not have come up to your standard of what constitutes a humanly good person, and yet they had in some way been adequately prepared for the spiritual experience.

One of those preparations is being a virgin; and being a virgin has no relationship whatsoever to being a humanly good person. It means to be absolutely pure and free of false concepts of God and God's creation, not entertaining idols, not worshiping false gods, and not entertaining a false sense of satisfaction. Spiritually, to be a virgin means to be free of false gods, false worship, preconceived ideas of God, prayer, and this universe. This is having a virgin mind, a mind that is clean of false spiritual concepts.

Furthermore, it is impossible for the spiritual birth to take place where there is not humility. Humility does not mean that false sense that thinks, "I am less than you, and I am less than anybody else in the world." No, it is a spiritual knowing that "I of my own self can be nothing; I of my own self can do nothing; I of my own self must be just a complete vacuum, a complete nothingness, dependent wholly, entirely, exclusively on God, the spiritual, the invisible."

When prayer and meditation are acts of humility, when they are acts of emptying yourself so that you can say, "Open my eyes that I may see; open my ears that I may hear; open my mind that I may know; open me inwardly to the divine presence"; there is the true humility that has set self aside.

Dying Out of a False Sense of Self

Scholars can lead us astray with the false knowledge that they have built up by living in books without spiritual enlightenment. They have taken out of the ancient wisdoms the great truth that it is necessary to die in order to be reborn, and because of that a religious belief has been built up which teaches that after a person dies a physical death he will be ready to go to heaven and meet God. That is almost as erroneous a translation of the truth as could possibly be made. The truth is that being reborn has nothing to do with the death of a physical sense of body; it has nothing to do with living a certain number of years and then leaving this earthly place to go to another place to find God.

The Master made it very clear that God is not to be found here or there, not on this side of the veil or on the other side of the veil: "The kingdom of God is within you."[2] If the kingdom of God is within you, that means *now*. The word in itself tells the story: right now the kingdom of God is within you. So according to the Master, you do not have to go any place to find it; and you do not have to wait any length of time to find it. The place is within you; the time is now.

Then what is meant by dying? In that is found the whole secret of your spiritual preparation. It is dying to your previous concepts, to your false concepts; it is dying to your false beliefs. Dying to a false concept of life is really the preparation.

Dying to Self-Preservation

In the human sense of life, you are told that self-preservation is the first law of nature. If you want to embark on that spiritual preparation, that is the first concept to which you must die. You have to give up the idea of self-preservation, because the self that you wish to perpetuate is that false sense of self which is keeping you from the God-experience.

All mystical literature reveals the truth of this. According to Alexis Carrel, out of the hundred thousand who went to Lourdes in a year, only fifteen were healed. Why those fifteen? He discovered that knowing they were incurable, knowing this was their last hope of saving their life, they gave up that chance, and instead of praying for themselves, they prayed for someone who they felt was worse off than they were or who they felt deserved healing in preference to themselves. In other words, instead of going there with this sense of self-preservation, they went there with a sense of self-sacrifice as much as to say, "If there is a spiritual power here to heal, instead of healing me, heal this friend of mine who has a family to take care of or some greater reason for living than I have." This is the death of the self that brings forth the revelation of God, and all fifteen of those who thus sacrificed themselves and were willing to die, lived.

Those fifteen lost their human sense of life and were reborn into spiritual harmony and perfection, and yet they did not die and go any place. On the contrary, what died was their disease. They themselves lived in harmony, in health, and went forth to show that when a person dies to the self, he is instantly reborn of the Spirit.

To enter the kingdom of God, therefore, means to die, but not to die in the sense of having a funeral and being buried, but dying in the sense of giving up one's self, surrendering that idea of self-preservation. The self that would be preserved is diseased mentally, physically, and morally. It is only in the surrender of that sense of self that the true Self is born, the Self that is health, the Self that is harmony, success, peace, joy, dominion.

The death that prepares you for heaven is not an experience in time or space: it is an experience in consciousness. It all takes place within your consciousness, and it takes place at the point of your readiness for that experience. The reason that a person is not always ready for the experience of attaining the God-realization, even after he believes he wants it, is that he does not recognize that there is an interval of preparation between the desire for God-experience and the realization itself. He does not recognize the importance of, or the necessity for, sloughing off the old concepts, and he believes that the kingdom of God can be added to his humanhood. He believes that he can be the same human being today that he was yesterday, and just add to his humanhood the kingdom of God.

The fifteen cases at Lourdes are definite proof that that is not true. When the person was willing to give up that self that wanted to live and agree that he did not care if he died, just as long as somebody else lived, he had gone through one form of preparation and readiness for the God-experience, albeit, an extreme one. In some measure, however, every person must recognize that no more of God is going to enter his consciousness than what he makes room for by emptying out some part of his human selfhood.

Forgiveness and Nonresistance as a Preparation for the Christ

The whole ministry of Christ Jesus was preparing his followers for the advent, for the experience of God. Jesus said, "Ye have heard that it hath been said, An eye for an eye, and a tooth for a tooth: But I say unto you, That ye resist not evil."[3] Right here is a state of preparation. You either make up your mind to give up seeking revenge, wanting to get even with somebody or believing that it is right to get even with somebody, or you give up any thought of preparing yourself for the spiritual experience. There has to be a time and a place in your consciousness— not a time and place in space—but a time and place in your consciousness when you forsake "an eye for an eye and a tooth for a tooth"; and are willing to take the next step of forgiving "seventy times seven."[4]

Giving merely lip service to that idea is not a preparation for the God-experience. The preparation is when, regardless of the offenses that are aimed against you day after day, you are able to forgive seventy times seven. "I forgive them. Father, do not punish them; forgive them their sins. They know not what they do." It sounds easy when you are preaching and teaching. The difficulty comes when you practice it.

A teacher must also be a practitioner, otherwise the teacher will never succeed as a teacher. Merely passing this good news on to somebody else is not really being a teacher; a teacher becomes a teacher only when in some degree he is living that idea of forgiveness, of not holding offenses perpetually against someone, and when he is to the best of his ability realizing, "Forgive them; forgive them. Do not punish, Father; forgive them, Father; they know not what they do."

You all know how virtuous you feel when you pray for your friends, your patients and students, tending to overlook the fact that Jesus made it clear that such prayer profiteth you nothing. Spiritually, there is no gain from praying for your friends, praying for your patients, or praying for your students. That, you have to do, but do not think there is any spiritual virtue in it.

The spiritual virtue comes when you are willing to sit down and pray for those who persecute you, personally, individually, nationally, internationally. It profits you nothing to pray for your friends. That does not mean you are to stop praying for them; it means not to expect to reap any spiritual reward for it or to expect to gain God because of it. You will begin to have the God-experience as you are able to pray for your enemies, for those that despitefully use you, and for the enemies of mankind, not pray that they be successful in overcoming the good, but pray that their eye be opened, pray that God reveal Himself to them, pray that they be forgiven their sins, that they awaken to the realities of life, to the joys, to the spiritual truth. There are many ways of praying for your enemies that in the last analysis will turn them into friends.

Put Up Your Sword

Throughout all the Master's experience on earth, he was showing you how to prepare yourself for God unfoldment. It is not that God is withholding Himself: it is you and I who are setting up barriers in consciousness that keep God from being fully revealed. We set up barriers just as we do when we put blinders on ourselves and then cannot see the sun or when we pull down the shades and keep it out. So it is we are keeping God out: God is not withholding Himself. We keep God out until we go through the preparatory stages that are revealed in the Sermon on the Mount that brings us eventually to where we can say with the Master when he was being arrested: "Put up again thy sword into his place: for all they that take the sword shall perish with the sword."⁵ That is the final act of the death of the self when we can say, "Put up again thy sword."

Those who live by physical means of protection will die; those who live by taking life from others will die. Put up your sword and trust the invisible presence, the God you have been seeking, the God that is closer to you than your very breath.

Can Civilization Survive?

Today you are living in a world that is going through one of its periodic upsets. The trials and tribulations of this age are the same trials and tribulations of every previous age. There have been tyrants and dictators throughout all ages; there have been business tycoons and capitalists, and there have been labor leaders under different names; and every form of evil that there is today has existed in one form or another. In all ages there have been persons with the experience of finding the Red Sea in front of them and Pharaoh's army in back of them. There have been very few generations since the beginning of time in which some nation or some group of nations has not been faced with a Red Sea in front of it and Pharaoh's army in back of it.

Looking around the nations of the world and see how many of them are facing Red Seas in front of them and Pharaoh's army in back of them. Look at the nations who at the present moment have no human way out of their dilemma. Regardless of how you may try to think, regardless of how the leaders of the nations have planned it, there are a number of nations, some of the major ones included, that have no human hope for survival. They are absolutely at the end of their time. Their particular Red Sea in front and Pharaoh's army in back have caught up with them, and they are in the middle.

As a matter of fact, there are those, including some of the great minds of today, who would say that civilization as a whole is at the point where it could be exterminated. Again, a Red Sea in front, and you can imagine what the particular Red Sea is; Pharaoh's army at the back, and you can imagine what form Pharaoh's army takes; and civilization caught in the middle with no human solution!

Is There a Spiritual Solution to the World's Problems?

Faced with the present world situation, you may ask yourself, "Even if it is true that there is a Red Sea in front of us and Pharaoh's army in back of us, even if there is not a human way out of the situations that confront us, is there a spiritual way out?" When that question enters your mind, you are almost at the point of the preparation necessary to receive the spiritual experience, where the answer lies. Not before, not before! As long as you have something human to hold onto, you are not at the point of preparation.

You have undoubtedly heard many times that it is easier to cure the incurable than it is the person with an ordinary sickness. Why? The person with a curable disease is most likely saying, "Well, of course, if God does not do it, I can still take some medicine or have a little surgery or resort to something else." The person who has reached his Red Sea and Pharaoh's army, however, and has been told, "There is no way for you but death," asks, "Yes, according to human knowledge, but what about divine knowledge?" In the moment that you throw aside your last lingering reliance on material help, then you are ready, and you are in a state of preparation.

In the Four Gospels, the Master has set forth the preparatory steps. If you are taking those steps, you are being led to a state of consciousness which looks out at this world and says, "I am no longer thinking about preserving my life. What I am thinking of now is preserving civilization and the world, the youth and the newborn." In past ages the middle-aged sent their children to die so that they could live the last ten or fifteen years of their span by depriving the young people of their whole lifetime. Now with a higher sense, the answer comes that the solution cannot be in sacrificing another young generation. Instead your prayer becomes, "God, stop thinking about me and let me stop thinking about me. How about civilization? How about mankind? How about this world? And how about the newborn? Is there a spiritual way out?"

Relinquishing Human Means of Survival

Stop thinking in terms of human self-preservation. Instead, think in terms of spiritual survival, spiritual law, spiritual life, a spiritual way or solution to the problems of the world. The very moment that you are able to put out of your mind the idea of human modes of survival and turn within and pray diligently, "What is the spiritual way of survival? What is the spiritual way of healing, the spiritual way of enriching, the spiritual way of good?" You are approaching the state of consciousness that has died to its belief in material means and you are entering the stage of rebirth and into the awareness of spiritual means.

The more you die to a search for material and mental means of survival, the closer you will come to spiritual realization. "My kingdom is not of this world."[6] The spiritual kingdom is not of this earthly plane, and therefore, if you want a solution from God, you have to turn away from thoughts of self-preservation to thoughts of God-preservation, spiritual-preservation, the dawning in consciousness of God's kingdom on earth.

There could be no greater preparation for your spiritual development than to acknowledge that this world has a Red Sea in front of it and a Pharaoh's army coming up behind it, and that between the two there is no human way out, and then turning within, asking, begging, pleading, "Father, show me the spiritual solution; show me the spiritual way. Show me how the Red Sea is to be opened; show me how Pharaoh's army is to destroy itself."

It is not that Pharaoh's army is to be destroyed or that a tunnel is to be built under the Red Sea. That is too easy. After you build the tunnel under the Red Sea, you have not solved anything. If you destroy Pharaoh's army, it pops up again under some other name. The armies of the enemy have appeared under different names from the days of Pharaoh to the days of Hitler and the days of Kruschev—all kinds of names for Pharaoh's army. It is not destroyed yet. It will not be destroyed, either, until it is destroyed spiritually. You will not destroy Pharaoh's army until you turn within and say, "Father, show us what Moses saw when the Red Sea opened and Pharaoh's army destroyed itself. Show us what the Hebrew prophet saw when he said, 'Do not fear the armies of the aliens, they have only temporal power; we have the Lord God almighty!'"

What did that Hebrew prophet see that was so powerful that the enemy destroyed itself, and his people did not have to go out and fight? What did he see? What did the Master see when he said, "Put up again thy sword into his place: for they that take the sword shall perish with the sword." What did he see? What was the way that he saw of salvation, of eternal life, of immortality? What was the way he saw of supplying multitudes without having storehouses or barns? Is there not a spiritual solution to every problem? Meditate on this and ponder this to prepare yourself for the advent of the Christ, the revelation in your consciousness of the way through the Red Sea and the armies of the Pharaohs.

TAPE RECORDED EXCERPTS
Prepared by the Editor

For almost two thousand years, Christmas has been celebrated to commemorate the birth of the Christ. But few persons have ever understood the meaning of that event and the real nature of the Christ. Long before the advent of the man Jesus, who embodied the Christ in Its fullness, however, Isaiah caught the vision of the nature of the Christ. The following excerpts shows something of his understanding of the Christ.

Isaiah's Vision of the Christ

"Isaiah probably had a greater vision of the Christ than any of the Old Testament prophets. Without any question or doubt, he not only saw Its coming, but the very nature and character of It. The Hebrews had always known of the coming of the Christ but they never knew Its nature. They thought of this Christ that would come as a man, but as a powerful man, a man who could be head of a government, a man who could be the head of an army, a man who through this God power would free them, not only from Rome, but probably from some of the malpractices of their church. In any event their dream of a Messiah was of a very powerful man, and a man who would right wrongs and give them their freedom. They might even have thought of him a little bit as a modern George Washington.

"But Isaiah knew better. Isaiah knew, even hundreds of years before the advent of the man Jesus, the exact nature of the Christ. Whether or not he knew that the Hebrews could never accept such a Messiahship, I do not know, but . . . in no uncertain terms he defined the Christ. He revealed the nature of the Christ and gave us the mission of It.

"We are making about the same mistakes that the Hebrews made. We also think of the Christ as a great power and like to think that when we achieve this Christ probably we also will have the power to go out and wield the big stick at all forms of sin, disease, death, and probably dictatorships, too. Most of the . . . so-called Christian world, the church world, has some lingering belief that if the Christ would only come It could do away with these dictatorships or evil powers that roam the earth.

"If we are to achieve harmony, first of all, in our minds and bodies, if we are to achieve harmony in our homes and in our relationships with each other, so that eventually this harmony will spread to the neighborhood, to the community, city, state, nation, and across the borders, it becomes necessary that we ourselves know the nature of the Christ and Its function. It would be well to begin with the revelation of Isaiah, the prophecy of Isaiah, and become familiar with the terms used by Isaiah for this Christ. Dwelling on that, it will make it possible to come more nearly to the realization of that which we are seeking. . . .

> Behold, a virgin shall conceive, and bear a son,
> and shall call his name Immanuel. . . .

> The people that walked in darkness
> have seen a great light:
> they that dwell in the land of the shadow of death,
> upon them hath the light shined.

> For unto us a child is born,
> unto us a son is given: and the government shall be
> upon his shoulder: and his name shall be called
> Wonderful, Counsellor, The mighty God,
> The everlasting Father, The Prince of Peace.

> Of the increase of his government and
> peace there shall be no end,
> upon the throne of David, and upon his kingdom,
> to order it, and to establish it
> with judgment and with justice

from henceforth even for ever. The zeal of the Lord
of hosts will perform this.

Isaiah 7:14, 9:2, 6,7

"In this reference to 'a virgin shall conceive,' you will understand that in this spiritual kingdom, . . . this Christ will not be
human, will not be material, but will be as that issuing forth
from a virgin, that which is, let us say, Self-made, Self-main-
tained, Self-sustained, as if out of Its own substance. And then
'Of the increase of his government and peace there shall be no
end'—not of the government of men on the earth and not of
peace of earth does he say there shall be no end. He says 'Of his
government and of his peace. . . .'

"In meditation dwell upon the idea of his government and
of his peace so that you can make the transition in your own
thought from the belief that you are seeking the Christ for the
purpose of changing your government and having a little more
human peace on earth."

Joel S. Goldsmith, "Isaiah 60: Prophecy and Vision of Isaiah,"
The Second 1953 New York Closed Class.

About the Series

The 1971 through 1981 *Letters* will be published as a series of eleven fine-quality soft cover books. Each book published in the first edition will be offered by Acropolis Books and The Valor Foundation, and can be ordered from either source:

ACROPOLIS BOOKS, INC.
8601 Dunwoody Place
Suite 303
Atlanta, GA 30350-2509
(800) 773-9923
acropolisbooks@mindspring.com

THE VALOR FOUNDATION
1101 Hillcrest Drive
Hollywood, FL 33021
(954) 989-3000
info@valorfoundation.com

Scriptural References and Notes

CHAPTER ONE

1. Luke 12:22.
2. II Chronicles 32:7,8.
3. I Samuel 17:39,46,47.
4. By the author.
5. John 4:32.
6. John 4:14.
7. John 6:35.
8. Psalm 91:10.
9. Psalm 91:1.
10. Psalm 23:2.
11. Galatians 2:20.
12. Matthew 5:39.
13. Matthew 13:24-30.
14. Psalm 23:4.
15. Psalm 139:7-10.

CHAPTER TWO

1. By the author.
2. Psalm 19:1.
3. John 5:30.
4. Psalms 37:25.
5. Exodus 3:5.
6. Luke 17:21.
7. Luke 15:31.
8. Ecclesiastes 11:1.
9. I Kings 17:13.
10. Matthew 6:12.
11. Romans 8:16,17.
12. Matthew 23:9.
13. John 8:58.
14. Mark 4:25.
15. Psalm 32:7.
16. Psalm 119:114.
17. Luke 12:22.
18. I Kings 19:12.
19. Philippians 2:5.
20. Hebrews 4:12.
21. John 10:30.
22. Galatians 2:20.

CHAPTER THREE

1. Galatians 2:20.
2. John 1:12.
3. II Corinthians 5:1.
4. Revelation 21:2.
5. Luke 23:35.
6. John 2:19.
7. Job 19:26.
8. John 8:11.
9. Luke 23:43.
10. John 7:24.
11. Mark 8:18.

CHAPTER FOUR

1. Mark 8:18.
2. Isaiah 54:17.
3. Exodus 3:5.
4. Psalm 23:4.
5. Luke 15:31.
6. Matthew 6:19.
7. John 5:30.
8. Mark 4:25.
9. Psalm 24:1.
10. Isaiah 45:2.
11. Matthew 11:3-5.
12. Romans 8:26.
13. Matthew 12:39.
14. Mark 16:17.
15. Matthew 10:37.
16. I Corinthians3:16.
17. Galatians 6:7.
18. Isaiah 1:18.
19. John 1:17.
20. Philippians 2:5.

CHAPTER FIVE

1. Exodus 3:14.
2. Alfred, Lord Tennyson.
3. Isaiah 45:2.
4. Job 23:14.
5. I John 4:4.
6. Luke 15:31.
7. Psalm 23:24.
8. I Thessalonians 5:17.
9. John 8:11.
10. Luke 23:43.
11. Matthew 26:40.

CHAPTER SIX

1. Psalm 42:11.
2. II Samuel 22:2.
3. John 12:32.
4. Philippians 2:5.
5. John 10:30.

CHAPTER SEVEN

1. Matthew 10:8.
2. Matthew 26:52.
3. II Chronicles 20:15.
4. Luke 23:34.
5. Isaiah 1:18.
6. Isaiah 44:2.
7. I Corinthians 6:19.
8. Isaiah 40:6.
9. Romans 8:13.
10. John 1:14.
11. Psalm 23:2.
12. John 15:5.
13. Galatians 2:20.
14. John 5:30.
15. John 14:10.
16. John 4:14.
17. John 4:32.
18. Matthew 7:7.
19. II Corinthians 12:9.

CHAPTER EIGHT

1. II Kings 2:9,10.
2. John 5:30.
3. John 14:10.
4. John 14:12.
5. Matthew 23:9.
6. Romans 12:2.
7. Isaiah 54:17.
8. Genesis 18:32.
9. Luke 12:32.
10. James 4:3.
11. Matthew 12:48,49.

12. Psalm 91:1.
13. Proverbs 3:6.
14. John 15:5,6.
15. Psalm 37:25.
16. Matthew 6:19.
17. Psalm 91:11.

CHAPTER NINE

1. Galatians 2:20.
2. Job 23:14.
3. Psalm 138:8.
4. Mark 8:18.
5. I Kings 19:12.
6. Isaiah 45:2.
7. Philippians 4:13.
8. II Corinthians 12:9.
9. Matthew 6:11.
10. John 6:35.
11. John 4:32.
12. John 4:14.
13. John 4:21.
14. Hebrews 4:12.
15. Luke 12:25,26.
16. John 1:14.

CHAPTER TEN

1. John 10:30.
2. John 18:36.
3. Matthew 7:14.
4. Isaiah 45:2.
5. Exodus 3:14.
6. John 14:27.
7. John 18:36.
8. John 7:24.
9. Romans 8:38,39.
10. Psalm 23:4.
11. Psalm 139:8.
12. Psalm 91:1.
13. Colossians 1:27.
14. Matthew 3:17.
15. Exodus 3:5.
16. Revelation 2:17.
17. John 2:32

CHAPTER ELEVEN

1. Matthew 5:45.
2. II Kings 4:2.
3. Luke 15:31.
4. John 10:30.
5. Psalm 23:4.
6. John 8:32.
7. Matthew 5:20.
8. Matthew 19:17.
9. Psalms 42:11.
10. John 9:25.
11. Galatians 6:7.
12. Isaiah 2:30.
13. Matthew 4:4.
14. Acts 10:34.

CHAPTER TWELVE

1. John 15:16.
2. Luke 17:21.
3. Matthew 5:38,39.
4. Matthew 18:22.
5. Matthew 26:52.
6. John 18:36.

Joel Goldsmith
Tape Recorded Classes
Corresponding to the
Chapters of this Volume

~

Tape recordings may be ordered from

THE INFINITE WAY
PO Box 2089, Peoria AZ 85380-2089
Telephone 800-922-3195 Fax 623-412-8766

E-mail: infiniteway@earthlink.net
www.joelgoldsmith.com
Free Catalog Upon Request